My Political Race

My Political Race

Parmjit Dhanda

Biteback Publishing

First published in Great Britain in 2015 by
Biteback Publishing Ltd
Westminster Tower
3 Albert Embankment
London SE1 7SP
Copyright © Parmjit Dhanda 2015

ISBN 978-1-84954-806-9

10 9 8 7 6 5 4 3 2 1

A CIP catalogue record for this book is available from the British Library.

Set in Adobe Garamond Pro

Printed and bound in Great Britain by
CPI Group (UK) Ltd, Croydon CR0 4YY

CONTENTS

FOREWORD

I KNEW PARMJIT DHANDA before he became an MP and I
know him now that his nine years representing Gloucester are
over. He has always been the same calm, rational and rather
suave young man, as polite as he is handsome.

Indeed, there was a hint of the cinema matinée idol about the
tall, slim union official who came to my ministerial office at
the old Department for Trade and Industry to talk about tele-
communications. At the end of our discussion, he told me that he
was keen to be adopted as the Labour candidate for Gloucester.
I knew many talented youngsters who wanted to be MPs, but
Parmjit was the son of an immigrant from India. He was also

a Sikh – that most peaceful and equitable of religions. Piara Khabra had become the first Sikh MP in 1992, but that was in Ealing Southall – a constituency with a substantial Sikh and Asian population.

Within a few years, Parmjit was back in the DTI as our government whip – the beginning of a ministerial career that was to take him to Education (as my Parliamentary Undersecretary of State) and to the Department for Communities and Local Government.

To demonstrate the odds he had to overcome, this book repeats an article from the *Gloucester Citizen*, published in 2000 – millennium year. It has dark echoes of an earlier age in its prediction that a dark-skinned, Indian Sikh couldn't possibly win 'in a cathedral city in the West Country that has a 5 per cent ethnic population ... and very few Sikhs'. It went on to cite the experience of John Taylor, the black barrister who, according to the article, had lost Cheltenham for the Conservatives primarily because of the colour of his skin.

Fortunately, Gloucester's citizens were more enlightened than the *Gloucester Citizen* and, just as Ben Bradshaw had proven in Exeter, race and sexuality were not the barriers to a parliamentary seat that bigoted opponents wanted them to be.

Parmjit certainly experienced prejudice and hatred. Indeed, the book begins with a horrendous incident (made only slightly comical by the demonstration of the laughable ignorance of its perpetrators). But this is an uplifting story of a young man who was at the heart of Labour's attempts to make Parliament more reflective of the population it serves and of the political events of the first tumultuous decade of this century.

This is an important piece of social documentary written by a man who has much more to offer to his party and his country.

Alan Johnson MP

CHAPTER 1

THE PIG'S HEAD

I T WAS THE day that changed everything. I like to think I'm a pretty tough cookie. I've been through a lot in my life. I've taken on the odds and I've won. I've also had to learn to deal with defeat.

I'm very proud of who and what I am. My roots are working class. My family roots lie in the villages of the Punjab. I'm from the Sikh faith and very proud of that too. I'm not dead yet, but I think I can be quite chuffed with some of my achievements. I was the youngest MP of the 2001 intake, and did it in a seat where I had no previous links. I won there even though internal and external forces told me I was the wrong colour to be Labour's candidate for the nation's bell-wether constituency. But I am also conscious that pride can be a dangerous thing, and that too much of it can be burst like a bloated balloon.

Maybe the pride is to blame for the unexpected impact the pig's head incident had on me and my sense of self-worth. Proud men can take the rough with the smooth. Surely proud men don't run away from a battle?

My own emotional response to this incident is not something I would have predicted. It got under my defences unlike anything that had preceded it. It highlighted my 'differentness' in a way that made me feel uncomfortable. It made me feel as if I'd never been truly accepted. Being different should be water off a duck's back to someone who's 6 ft 3 tall and wrapped in brown skin, while representing a community that is over 90 per cent white.

But this was different. It wasn't on my terms. I didn't have control of events. And, significantly, it was no longer just about me. I could deal with uncomfortable situations that impacted on me. Proud men can defend themselves. But what if you're not around – travelling, away for days on end – and you can't defend those closest to you? And what if you can't define or understand what you're defending them from? If people are willing to do odd, bizarre and frankly frightening things around a woman at home, largely alone, and your children, then what do you do? We were safer when I was part of the establishment. But I was no longer part of the public establishment or the Labour Party establishment. We were now on our own. Proud men, after all, can protect their wives and their children. But when your support networks break down, you're left vulnerable and alone.

Zac hadn't quite turned five and little Maxi was in nappies. In the twenty-first century, I would never have thought I'd have to shield them from racism. And if I couldn't, what did that say about me?

• • •

It wasn't a happy time. My full-time job for the trade union meant leaving Gloucester on a Monday morning and living in a flat in Kennington during the week, coming home on Thursday night. It was tough for Rupi and the boys. Max was only a year old and Zac just four when Labour lost the 2010 election, and they would have to adapt to my being away, without the recesses and flexibility I'd once had, to see more of those in the constituency.

I always knew it would happen some day, but I could already feel the arm of the Labour hierarchy, which had once been draped firmly around my shoulders, slowly slipping away. Texts to those who used to tell me how fabulous I was now went unanswered.

There's nothing more 'ex' than an ex-MP.

And it teaches you who your friends truly are. All those hand-written notes you receive when you've just lost (I've kept every one of them); all those offers of help – 'We must do everything we can to bring you back, we miss you…' – but where do those people all go when you really need them? A few of them are genuine and go the extra mile to call you, advise you and help you. But most promise the earth and will then turn their backs on you when it's crunch time. Politics is a brutal game where the wounded and the fallen are often left behind on the battlefield while the army marches on.

Perhaps being elected so young, and in the first seat I genuinely tried for, was a curse. Winning aged twenty-nine was great. But losing at thirty-eight – with a young family and a mortgage – was a harder blow than I ever anticipated. I'd put so much of my 'self' into those nine years and I took the loss personally, even though I knew I shouldn't.

The journeying to London and back left too much time to dwell on election defeat and whether my career in politics had come to a permanent and premature end.

On the upside, things could only get better. Surely we'd hit rock bottom.

. . .

8.15 a.m., Sunday 12 December 2010, Gloucester. In the Dhanda household, Sunday means a lie-in for Rupi, while I get turfed out of bed to make breakfast. Nothing extravagant: some warm croissants in the oven and a pan of Indian tea brought to simmering point on the gas hob.

The kids had settled down to eat in the dining room, which was open-plan with the kitchen. I finished off the tea while keeping half an eye on our young ruffians, making sure they were actually eating instead of flicking food or kicking each other under the table. Sons!

Zac and Max

Max had adopted the seat at the head of the table as his own, due to the fact the baby seat had fitted in nicely there. Although he'd out-grown it, he was attached to his place at the head of the group and had his booster cushion fixed there now. It was also the regular place for the plastic mat under his chair – to protect the carpet from his cast-offs – but the stains on the carpet showed it had been a rather unsuccessful project. As I looked over Maxi's head, I could see one of our two cars in the front drive and about a third of our front gar-den as it sloped gently towards a hedge – which separated our home from the brook that gave the house its name: Brookside. All this sounds rather more rural than it was – just a mile from Gloucester city centre, it lay on the corner of the busy Painswick Road and the sleepier cul-de-sac called The Wheatridge.

I could see that it was a rather grey and dull day outside. The house, although having a good-sized hedge to shield the ground floor from the main road, was not the best place for a very visible MP to live in his constituency (or ex-MP, as I had been for six months now). Everybody seemed to know where our home was. From con-stituents' comments like 'I saw you hanging up curtains, Mr MP!' to 'Drove past your house and didn't see your cars – were you away at the weekend?', I soon became aware that the house was not located in the most secure place and we should have thought more carefully about where we were going to make our family home, even though we had needed to find one in a hurry.

The flat in Kingsholm I had lived in, from the time I was adopted as Labour's candidate in 2000, had been perfect for me. A couple of years later, Rupi and I had got together and it suited us just fine too. Then we did something rather irresponsible. Bearing in mind this was historically one of the most marginal seats in the land, planning a family was not on the agenda for us until after the 2005 general election was settled – at the earliest. But, within a week of the 2005 campaign ending, Rupi realised she was pregnant. It was great news, but I'm not sure I'd have been so cheery about it had I lost my job a few days earlier. I must advise any aspiring MPs reading this book that, unless you're financially secure, try not to get pregnant, or get your partner pregnant, during an election campaign. So, we sold the flat and bought our first family home – Brookside – just in time for Zac's arrival on New Year's Day 2006.

As I poured out the tea on that Sunday morning in 2010, I listened to Zac's chit-chat on the phone to my dad (his grandpa). On Sunday mornings, before, after and sometimes during breakfast, the kids would catch up with Mum and Dad on the phone.

When the doorbell rang, I knew something wasn't right. Who would be at the door at 8.15 a.m. on a Sunday? It was pretty unusual for people to turn up unannounced at our home and, when it did happen, it often spelled trouble. When I was away in Parliament a year earlier, a woman with mental health problems was banging on the door in the middle of the night, demanding a meeting with me. It was a case my office had been dealing with, but she should not have been banging on the door of our home in the early hours. Rupi dealt with it, but she was quite shaken at the time. She should never have answered the door. People in the state that woman had been in can be so unpredictable. Whenever I was in staying in London, I would dread the late-night calls from our Gloucester home. On more than one occasion, I had to scramble helpful friends out in their pyjamas in the middle of the night to check that Rupi and the kids were OK when the bell or the alarm were sounding. People hanging around the place, break-ins, a smashed car windscreen and battered fences were all signs that things weren't right. It can happen to anyone but it's not wise for people in public life to make a fuss – you'll only get a reputation as a whiner. I was usually away when it happened, and it was happening a little too often for comfort.

I can recall an occasion when I was at home, and a group of angry residents (about seven of them) turned up on the doorstep. Zac was a babe in arms back then and was clinging to me when I opened the door. The mob weren't intimidating but they simply refused to wait for the weekend to end to come and see me in my constituency office. Apparently, some kids had set fire to a hedge and the residents weren't happy that the police hadn't put their best brains on the case. I was sympathetic, but hardly well placed to take up their case in my pyjamas, with a teething baby in my arms. But we talked (or rather, I listened for about a quarter of an hour). They rewarded my patience by putting a letter in the newspaper the following week basically telling the world they'd been to our house, giving its location, and stating that I wouldn't put out their fire.

So when I heard the doorbell that Sunday morning, my first instinct was to be ready to politely tell whoever was at the door that, if their hedge was on fire, they'd lost their pills or Billy hadn't been accepted by one of the grammar schools, then it was no longer my role in life to sort it out. I was no longer the MP after all, so surely the upside of defeat was that we could live in relative peace?

I left the kids to chitter-chatter and went to answer the front door. Straight away I knew this was something different. There was no anger or malice about this lady. I don't know her name, or how old she was. I'd imagine she was in her fifties. I do remember that, despite her obvious distress, she had a kind face. It's one of those things you look out for as a politician. Who's nice and who's sympathetic? Are they the kind of person who'd smile back if you smiled at them?

She had a dog on a lead. It was pulling away from her, trying to drag her away from my doorstep. 'It's horrible,' she said. She was struggling to hold it all together, so I knew this was going to be bad news, whatever it was. 'They've left something horrible for you behind your car.' She trembled throughout. The rest of our meeting was something of a blur. I can't really recall what else she said, just her state of distress. She may have mentioned something about not wanting children to see it. I don't recall her departure either, but I know she wasn't around when I went outside. Other than saying it was horrible, I don't even recall her telling me what it was. She said the dog had found it.

I thanked her and said I'd deal with whatever it was, but my first thought was Zac and Max, who were having breakfast with their backs to the window in the dining room overlooking our front garden.

I called up to Rupi to come down and look after the kids so I could go outside, in my gown and trainers, to take a look. She'd heard the door bell and came straight down.

I went out not really knowing what to expect. As I walked around the back of the car I saw it. There's no mistaking a severed pig's head any which way you look at it. With my back to the road, facing our front door, I was face-to-face with it, looking up at me. My own calmness and internal matter-of-factness surprised me to the extent that I crouched down to take a closer look. My first concern was the view from the dining room: I didn't want Rupi or the kids to see it. Thankfully, as I learned later from our own grainy CCTV footage, though it had been placed on top of our SUV (a Hyundai Tucson) to face us when we looked out of the house, as whoever did it ran away, it rolled off the roof and into a dip in the tarmac that largely prevented the street from seeing it.

You can't help but stare at something like that, however distasteful it is. I felt like it summed up my life at that time. Just when I thought we'd hit rock bottom, this happened. I didn't feel angry – I felt more than a bit sad. Have I changed nothing in my life? To my knowledge, there'd never been a UK minister of Indian parentage until Tony Blair promoted me. I'd worked so hard for this constituency and I felt my record of achievement was the best they'd ever had. It was almost comical that they thought the best way to offend me was by leaving a pig's head on my drive because they assumed I was a Muslim. The subtlety of these people to know the difference between a Sikh and a Muslim would have been a bit much to expect, I guess.

I could have gone back in time to my school days, when we were all pakis or wogs – what did it matter anyway? We were all the same and just as likely to get clouted in the playground by a complete stranger.

Nine years. I gave you my heart and soul for nine years. And you gave me this.

I needed to get on with what had to be done. Shield the kids; do whatever necessary with the police to get the head moved and make sure the word didn't get out. I did not want the incident to cloud nine successful years in Parliament, serving this community, as well as three ministerial jobs, serving this country. Maybe one day, I thought, I'd be ready to talk about it. When I did, it would not be as a victim and it would not be on *their* terms.

I told Rupi, who took it as I knew she would: with a shrug and that look I'd seen many times before – the 'how much more?' look. It was also a 'we need to go, leave this place behind' look. Letting go of the place I loved so much would be more than a wrench for me. But, at the same time, I needed to feel a sense of control, a sense that I could protect my family from this rubbish. I didn't want my bright and inquisitive five-year-old to be asked about this kind of stuff at school. Racism is something my generation had to face up to every day at school thirty years ago. It isn't meant to be part of the modern-day script.

I'd like to put on record our thanks to the local constabulary, who were terrific that day and on the many occasions we needed them before and after my time as MP. Perhaps it was a slight overkill on the day, as two police cars, followed by an inspector and then a police photographer, arrived to do their work – small wonder the neighbours were ringing within half an hour and rallying round, putting things into some perspective. The deputy chief constable, a lovely guy by the name of Ivor Twydell, phoned me. We'd worked together during the 2007 Gloucester floods, as well as on the successful bid for resources for the new police HQ. I asked him to tone things down a bit because the local newspaper was difficult and we wanted to keep things quiet. So the police cars were moved off the drive, the pig's head was taken away and the officers were called off from doing any door-to-door stuff.

We gave our statements. Things moved on. But something had changed forever. I had, after all, my pride.

CHAPTER 2

THE LONG ROAD TO VICTORY

ONE OF THE biggest days in the history of the Labour Party was 1 May 1997. For eighteen years the Labour Party had toiled in opposition, at times broken.

I have vague memories of Mrs Thatcher storming to power in the 1979 general election, but I was only seven at the time. My parents were Labour voters, so I shared their concerns about the world I was to grow up in. Things are quite binary at that age, but racism was a big thing in my life as it was very much alive in the classroom and the playground. With the National Front on the rise, there was conflict on the streets, and racist abuse regularly poured out of the windows of passing cars in areas like ours. This was mirrored in the playground, where paki-bashing and racism were rife, handed down from parent to child and leading to fisti-cuffs all too often. It was just a part of life.

I recall not being particularly thrilled about the Tories winning, but I was only seven at the time of the election – I would have just gone back to playing with my Action Man. Well, it wasn't actually an Action Man but a cheap imitation from Southall Broadway called Johnny Jackson. It didn't have eagle eyes or military khakis, but Mum used the sewing machine to make some outfits for him with off-cuts from the Indian suits she made. Sari material is not ideal for covert combat and I must have had the world's first cross-dressing imitation Action Man, but I still thought he was great.

Come the 1983 general election, the Labour Party was in the mire. The party manifesto was a left-winger's dream, calling for mass-scale nationalisation, tax-squeezing the rich until their pips squeaked and unilateral nuclear disarmament. Our manifesto was also dubbed the longest suicide note in history. The Labour Party was enjoying some amazing punch-ups: it was riven with ideological splits and personality feuds, which made for great television but bad politics. Michael Foot, a lovely man with great intellect but a bad dress sense, was our leader, making donkey jackets famous for all the wrong reasons. I can recall sitting cross-legged in the school hall at Yeading Primary School, our teacher Mrs Brown shaking her head and loudly tut-tutting as we watched TV footage of a remembrance ceremony at the national cenotaph. Michael Foot's attire didn't impress Mrs Brown.

The Tories were heading for a landslide, backed by the nationalistic tide of victory over the Argentinians in the Falklands a year before the election. As a ten-year-old in class 3A, I got myself in a spot of bother over the Falklands War. Our form tutor, Mrs Alexander, was a softly spoken, God-fearing woman, who liked to start and end the day with prayers. For a school that was becoming increasingly Sikh, Hindu and Muslim in its intake, it was amazing how much time we spent writing about Joseph, Mary, the Philistines and Moses. Not necessarily in that order. When the Falklands War kicked off, Mrs Alexander, as per the usual routine, asked us to put our chairs on the table at the end of the school day, close our eyes and get ready to pray. On this occasion, she asked us to pray for 'all those young British soldiers who were off fighting for our country in the Falkland Isles'. I put my hand up. She ignored me. But I kept my hand up, now on tiptoes. Maybe she hadn't noticed me because I was at the back of the classroom. Around me, the boys and girls of green table started to twitch nervously at what I was about to say.

'Yes, Parmjit,' Mrs Alexander said. 'What's the matter?'

'Miss, I don't think the young Argentinian people want to be out there fighting either. They are just doing what they're told to do and might die as well. Shouldn't we pray for them too?'

Silence. I don't think Mrs Alexander had quite anticipated that one. There was a sharp intake of breath on green table, which felt like a lonely place as they all stared at their feet, although a few of my other classmates *were* looking at me. Skinhead Glenn of blue table was particularly focused on me as he drew a finger across his throat in a slashing gesture.

'Yes,' said Mrs Alexander, not entirely enthusiastically. 'And let us pray for all of the soldiers...'

As we left class to go home after prayers, my mate Raj asked: 'Have you got a death wish or something, Parmj? You're going to get us all bashed up, mate!'

I certainly wasn't the kind of kid who'd keep Hansard under the bed, partly because I didn't know what it was, but when a decision was made that Yeading Primary School would have a *John Craven's Newsround*-style mock election, I was asked if I'd be the Labour candidate. Labour was wiped out in 1983 as the Tories swept to victory by over 140 seats. But, in the Hayes & Harlington constituency, Yeading Primary School went red on a blue night for the nation. Ranjeev Sekhon made her case for the SDP politely; Barry O'Sullivan held up a picture from the *Daily Mail* of a litter-strewn street to emphasise his point about 'Labour danger' on behalf of the Conservatives; but I was too popular in class 3A to be defeated. Barry and I had to be separated by Mrs Brown when I took issue with my classmate's prop from the *Daily Mail*, but things settled down. An eleven-year-old's simplistic logic about the need to create jobs and money for our parents by building more houses was enough for me to win by a landslide (and it was probably more coherent than the actual Labour Party manifesto of 1983), although the key factor was actually that the demographics in Yeading were changing and the class looked more like me than Barry – coupled with me sharing out my Smarties at playtime. Even then I had to challenge one of the teachers for trying to put an SDP vote on top of my Labour pile, threatening to steal my majority (my first experience of voter fraud).

Come 1987, the Labour Party was being rejuvenated by Neil Kinnock and the in-fighting was settling down. But the party was not about to regain the trust of the British people so soon and it was roundly beaten by over 100 seats. The path to victory for Labour would be a long one.

The Thatcher days had really politicised me and I had started to get to know some people in the local Labour Party in Hayes. Over time, inspired by Neil Kinnock, I would join the national party. But I was more supporter than activist. At Mellow Lane Comprehensive, the sixth-formers put up candidates in a mock election that the rest of us were allowed to vote in. I was very happy to wear stickers and illegally fly-post a few signs around the school for the Labour candidate, but that was hormones as much as anything: I had a terrible crush on her. She showed her affection by hugging me in front of my pals after her victory, for which I was more grateful than she ever need know.

Although, nationally, 1987 was a bleak election for Labour, I was confident that 1992 would be different.

In between the 1987 and 1992 general elections I had become a full and proper card-carrying member of the Labour Party. From standing out in the street with a collection bucket for striking ambulance workers to knocking on doors for local council candidates, I had made the first steps to becoming an 'activist'. I was a bit wary of some of the other activists though. They didn't all seem, well ... normal. There is something about political parties that attracts unusual and fanatical people – and they speak a language of their own.

Aged sixteen, I turned up at my first Labour Party meeting. It was the AGM of the Yeading branch of the Hayes & Harlington Constituency Labour Party (CLP). I was ready to join my new band of brothers and sisters in the Yeading ward, to storm the barricades and remove the evil Mrs T. from power! As it turned out, I shyly sat and listened to half a dozen men and women in a quiet living room in Willow Tree Lane, drinking tea and petting the cat while the comrades spoke in code. They went on about what the GC delegates to the EC would be reporting back at this AGM. And then there'd be a report from the LGC delegate who had the hump because: 'How was he going to be on the LGC if he wasn't a delegate to the GC? And he really needed to be on the LGCEC as well as the LGC.'

It would take me years to decipher these codes, but for months to come I wouldn't be able to tell my GC from my elbow. What were they talking about? I sat sipping my tea, occasionally nodding and petting the cat and trying to go unnoticed.

After two hours, and as I struggled to stay awake, I noticed we were on the final agenda item: 'The AGM election of officers.'

One of the officers read from his notes: 'According to CLP standing orders, we shall need a full slate of officers elected at the AGM of the Yeading branch of the CLP.' Before I could leg it out of the room, I'd been cornered by my new comrades and appointed vice-chair of an organisation I knew nothing about. So, my first lesson of Labour Party politics was learnt: when a new, young and unsuspecting person turns up at a meeting, dump as much responsibility on them as possible before they know what's going on. For, if they know too much, they'll probably say no.

By 1990 I was off to the University of Nottingham, but I kept my party membership in Hayes & Harlington. Other than the occasional meeting of the Labour club, student union politics wasn't for me – there were far too many other distractions at university for me to get involved in. On my returns to west London, I'd dip back into what I considered 'real politics' in a seat Labour was destined to win at the 1992 general election. Or were we?

The Tories threw us a curve-ball in the run-up to the general election by deposing Margaret Thatcher in 1990. When John Major replaced her, perhaps too many people felt the battle had already been won. I thought we were going to win. I returned from Nottingham to be a part of it in Hayes on polling day to knock up for our new candidate, a fresh-faced John McDonnell, who had arrived in the constituency after being beaten to the Hampstead & Highgate seat nomination by Glenda Jackson, and was now all set to become our Labour MP.

I was no expert, not yet anyway, but something didn't feel right on polling day. The national polls had narrowed in recent days, although not by enough to stop us, but things in the Yeading ward seemed haphazard. Pure adrenalin and emotion had got the better of organisation. Some sharp-suited people who I'd never seen before, but who I don't think were party employees, were running around barking orders as if we were in the trenches. At one point, with an hour to go before polls closed, I heard a strong Indian accent over a megaphone attached to a passing car. The Tory MP was an incredibly right-wing man called Terry Dicks. The megaphone voice with the strong Indian accent had a very sophisticated, persuasive and loud message. It went something like this: 'Vote Telly Dicks, vote Telly Dicks, vote Telly Dicks. Please. Please.' Repetitively.

I wouldn't worry too much about that, I thought. And I carried on diligently working through my sheet of addresses to get out the Labour votes that were needed to see John become our local MP.

But the megaphone had spooked a member of the loud-suited brigade, who was walking down Berwick Avenue with a megaphone of his own, and he ordered people to get him a car so he could follow Mr Telly Dicks's number one fan and shout him down through the streets of Hayes, Harlington and beyond.

I finished off and went home tired but quite happy. The exit polls predicted a small but working majority for Labour. As the night wore on and the results came in, the predictions changed. Labour was to be the largest party without an overall majority. Then the Tories looked like they were to be the largest party. Tired and fed up, I went to bed with the consolation that at least we'd won in my home constituency of Hayes & Harlington, just as we had done when I was the candidate in the *John Craven's Newsround* election nine years earlier.

Then I woke up to the news that the Conservatives had an overall majority of twenty-one and had held Hayes with a majority of fifty-three. I was mortified.

In the years to come, I would yearn to do something about it.

CHAPTER 3

BACK TO THE BEGINNING

MOST OF US are shaped by our parents and their experiences. Although I wasn't born until 1971, in many respects my political race begins in 1962, when Dad left his village in Punjab, India, to come to London to start a new life. He was just eighteen years old.

Dad's uncle sponsored his application to come here, and put him up in a room at 106 Townsend Road, just off Southall Broadway, west London. In those days there was not a single Asian shop on Southall Broadway. It's now home to one of the largest Sikh Punjabi communities outside of India, and many other communities

21

too. There was a shop in Old Southall that used to supply Dad, his roommate and many like them by making weekly visits on Saturdays to deliver traditional Indian food. But, for much of that time, Dad lived off tinned rice pudding – putting it in a pan of boiling water to heat it up. The Pot Noodle of its day, I guess.

So many people of my generation hear the story about how their fathers came here with just a few quid in their pockets and only the clothes they stood in. But it's true: in Dad's case it was two quid. He left behind the rural poverty of a farm in a Punjabi village (a village appropriately called Dhanda) for a different kind of poverty in west London – but with his dreams intact. In time, he was joined in England by his parents and his three younger siblings – two brothers and a sister.

He arrived on 11 January 1962 and was in work within days – he started on 31 January as a machine tool-setter at FT Fridges. His first day saw one of the heaviest snowfalls for very many years, but by bus and foot he made it into work and served the company until he was made redundant in 1979. Redundancy was a shock to the system for him; I can still recall the tough days that followed it.

At home we developed a regular routine. Every Sunday morning we'd drink Indian tea, play cards with Mum and Dad in their bedroom and discuss current affairs. There was no history of membership of a political party in our household until I joined Labour at the age of seventeen, but we were always immensely politically aware. We were wary of the National Front and indeed the right wing of the Tory Party, who didn't appear that different from each other in those days.

Racism was rife in the 1970s. Recently I asked Dad about his experiences of racism in the early days in the 1960s. He shrugged his shoulders and said, 'Well, what would you expect, son?' On one of his first outings from Townsend Road to Southall Broadway, he recalls that a little boy saw him and ran off in floods of tears to his mother and father. That wasn't racism but fear of the unknown; in this case, fear of Dad's beard and turban. Dad shaved his beard and cut his hair that day in order to be accepted. From my father's recollection, all of the young Sikh men who came from India at that time were clean-shaven when they arrived or soon became clean-shaven to fit in.

In order to get on they needed to fit in, not make waves. People often say to me: 'Why aren't Sikhs involved in politics – why don't they push harder for things and get their share of funding or positions in public life?' It doesn't come naturally to us; we don't generally make a hullabaloo. We just graft and get on.

But beyond the chats about current affairs over tea on Sunday mornings, I was becoming politicised, even though I wasn't aware of it.

The biggest factor in my politicisation was my mother Satvinder Kaur Dhanda. Mum and Dad were betrothed when she was eleven years old and he was sixteen. They'd never met and wouldn't do so until Dad sent for her in September 1965 when he was twenty-three and she was eighteen. She was from a village called Salempur. The conduit of their betrothal was in the army with my paternal grandfather.

For people like us born in the UK, this seems an odd arrangement, to say the least. But it was custom and practice in the motherland. The first time Dad saw Mum was when he collected her at Heathrow Airport and she was accompanied by an uncle and cousin. Mum moved into Dad's former home on Townsend Road in Southall. Dad had saved enough money within his first two years here to move into a home he had just bought – albeit with plenty of lodgers there to help him pay the mortgage – at 32 Beresford Road, just a few streets away. The three-bedroom terrace cost him £3,500. In December 1965, in a room on Townsend Road, they had a simple Sikh wedding ceremony and Mum then moved into the Beresford Road home with Dad.

My parents' wedding in 106 Townsend Road   *My parents as newlyweds*

They were a strikingly good-looking couple and, luckily for them, they turned out to be a good match for each other. In October 1966, my big brother Baljinder was born. Two years later came my sister Parminder and the family was complete. Then there was a mishap. My mother once let it slip to me that with a boy and a girl already there were no plans for any more little Dhandas. But, in September 1971, weighing in at 9lb 4oz, there I was. As the youngest, I was destined to be somewhat indulged and allowed to do my own thing. But I think my siblings would probably say I was spoilt rather than indulged, and they're probably right.

With my siblings

Nearly fifty years since their arrival in England, with three children and seven grandchildren, Mum and Dad can reflect on a good and fulfilling life together, which in part was covered by the BBC in a documentary called *Big Dreams*. The programme was about their generation and people like me, who broke through some glass ceilings in such an unlikely way considering our roots. Watching the documentary taught me something about myself and how I became politicised. Mum, who has always been the feisty one in the family, would go on to have a very strong influence on my path.

· · ·

Big Dreams was aired by the BBC in 2002, the year after my election as MP. They got me to talk about the things that had mattered to me when I was young and the things that had worried me growing up – like Dad's job as an HGV driver doing the night shifts in his truck from London to Liverpool or Manchester and back. He would have to help unpack the cargo at the other end when they were short-staffed before making the long return journey home again. I worried a lot about that as a boy. It was a lot of driving, late at night and a lot of physical work. He was clearly unhappy himself. But you've got to work, haven't you?

Then one night he had an accident. The truck went through the central reservation of the M1 and crashed into the hard shoulder on the other side. He was badly shaken, but thankfully he was OK and nobody was hurt. But he was lucky. And he wasn't the only one to be shaken up by it.

It got me thinking about how hard life was for some groups of people; and how easy it seemed to be for others. For people like us, it was always going to be a struggle. And I've never been able to shake the chip off my shoulder about working conditions, lack of quality schools, poorer health and lower life expectancy for people who grew up in my working-class neighbourhood versus folk who have better life chances due to the good fortune of where they were born and the size of their parents' bank balance. By forcing me to recount stories about growing up, *Big Dreams* brought to my focus the experiences that had shaped me, which was pretty handy for a new MP.

In 1974, we moved a few hundred yards from Beresford Road to a house in Hayes, where Mum and Dad still live and where I grew up – I lived there from the age of three until I was prised from the house by my selection by the Gloucester Labour Party aged twenty-eight. *Big Dreams* took me on the short walk from our house in Hayes to the Hambrough Tavern pub over the Hayes/ Southall Bridge. The pub sat atop the bridge.

I recalled cowering in my bedroom, listening to the riots and then seeing the smoke rise as our local pub was burnt down in 1977. A skinhead band called the Four Skins (you couldn't make it up) had come to our pub. *Our* pub of all places. This was the place where the Asian community felt safe having a pint at a time when the National Front was on the rise. It was a racially charged era; Blair Peach was killed at an anti-Nazi march in Southall about that time too.

The Four Skins brought coachloads of skinhead supporters to watch their gig at the Hambrough. I was six, but I can remember the fear that gripped the community at the time. Stories circulated door to door and over the telephones that a Sikh girl had had the plaits cut off her hair by a skinhead with a Stanley knife. Women and children were urged to stay inside while the men readied themselves to defend their patch.

Before long, National Front members had left the burning pub and were throwing stones from the top of the bridge that rained down on Southall. The police tried to form a barrier between the men and the Asian community below but, looking up the bridge from Hayes or Southall to the smouldering pub, all you could see was a group of skinheads goading you and backed up by police with truncheons forcing you back. The physical alignment of the National Front and the Metropolitan Police – however unintended it may have been – made the situation even more volatile.

The first road at the bottom of the bridge – the one that people were being forced down as they took shelter from the missiles raining down – was Beresford Road. My mum's brother and his young family now owned 32 Beresford Road, but my uncle was one of the many people who were rounded up by police that night. He's not an aggressive man and I do believe he was just looking to see what all the fuss was about. That's his story anyway, and he's stuck to it.

Mind you, my younger cousin Ginz (his son) has never been able to stay out of trouble. He was just a toddler at the time of the riots. Two local rival Asian gangs – the Tooti-nungs and the Holy Smokes – had come together that night for the common cause. Many of them were tearing down Beresford Road to get away from the bridge; others were sheltering there before bursting out to throw Molotov cocktails made from glass milk bottles (those were the days of doorstep milk delivery). As the milk bottles ran out and people back-peddled past 32 Beresford Road, I'm told toddler Ginz managed to open the front door by himself and was 'helpfully' passing glass milk bottles through a gap in the garden gate to passers-by – until my grandmother got her hands on him!

So, although I didn't see it as such at the time, I was surrounded by political forces and political events. The Southall riots, the struggle to be accepted and the desire to get on in life no matter what was thrown at us were becoming a part of my local community's DNA. All this would also shape my future.

CHAPTER 4

MOPS AND BRICKBATS

I F YOU DON'T speak a word of English and you have no qualifications then what do you do? My mother was in this predicament, as were quite a lot of young women just like her.

So, they became cleaners in the NHS. The three words of English my mum could speak when she started work at Hillingdon Hospital were, 'You do it!' – a phrase she would use if she suffered any racist taunts about people like her coming to this country to 'nick British jobs'.

Those three words from my mother, with her mop thrust in their recipient's direction, would be enough to send anyone packing. She might be a slender and demure-looking lady, but she has never lost the ability to fire off a shrill salvo. Believe me. Despite her limited vocabulary, my mother's ability to be gobby was noted by those around her, who saw her as a good first line of defence in most things that happened in life.

The trade union that represented the cleaners was called NUPE – the National Union of Public Employees – and is these days a big part of what has become Unison. NUPE became aware of Satvinder and asked her to be a shop steward. She wasn't convinced at first, but they promised to send her on courses to expand her vocabulary. They needed someone in touch with the new cadre of staff who were doing menial jobs. Whenever the shifts changed at the hospital, one group of cleaners containing a high proportion of Asian women was replaced by another group containing an even higher proportion of Asian women.

Mum training to be a union rep

One of the union's branch secretaries, whom Mum would get to know well, was a young left-wing firebrand called Bernie Grant. Mum often acted as a translator for Bernie when one of her colleagues had a problem at work. Bernie went on to become the MP for Tottenham many years later.

So, I was destined to be sent to school wearing NUPE badges from a very young age and armed with NUPE pens and pencils. I didn't know what it meant, but the badges were gold and shiny and became badges of honour in my infancy.

As a teenager, I wasn't destined to be one of the lucky kids who would land summer work at the town hall behind the desk for a princely sum. But Mum was always on hand to get me something at one of the local hospitals – portering or cleaning for £2.40 an hour. I remember groaning my way through a day at Ealing Hospital when I had spent the entire time reaching up to hang curtains on the bays in the wards. One of the Irish builders stopped me for a chat and a catch-up, which was a blessed break, and we got talking about the A levels I was doing and the university I was hoping to go to.

'Well, cheer up, son!' he said. 'You'll look back on this one day and you'll remember it was jobs like these that made you. You're doing it for the summer. Remember, I'll be doing it until I retire.'

He was, of course, right. Without my ever realising it, my experiences, my senses, my surroundings and my upbringing were sending me on a political journey.

The cheek-by-jowl nature of the lives of my parents' generation created amazing ties within the community that still endure today. As a kid it was a source of frustration, particularly when I was dragged out shopping with my mother every Saturday and we couldn't get to the next street corner without Mum being caught up in long conversations with people we knew/were related to/had lodged with etc. in our closely networked and growing community. The change in the few short years from Dad's arrival in 1962 was immense and would one day change Southall and Labour Party politics in an extraordinary way.

Later in life I would learn just how close these bonds were in my political life.

CHAPTER 5

LABOUR'S MAN
... IN BASINGSTOKE

I FOUND IT IMPOSSIBLE breaking into Parliament. No MP would have me as a researcher, as hard as I tried. In fact, the first time I ever stepped foot in the chamber of the House of Commons was after I was elected. I figured forcing my way in as an MP would be the only way to get a job in the place.

I don't tick a lot of the boxes you need to tick to become a politician. I did a degree in electrical and electronic engineering at the University of Nottingham. I was one of three people from my year group at our comp who managed to sneak into a red-brick institution – and one of them didn't count because it was the impossibly intelligent Richard Crabtree, who was a quirk of nature. Everyone knows a Richard Crabtree. He's the kid who got ten As in his GCSEs and featured in the local newspaper, then managed all As in his A levels and went to Cambridge. He may not have been the most gifted on the dance floor and he wasn't going to captain the football team, but he was as clever as clever could be and was also very generous in sharing his coursework with the rest of us, for which we were immensely grateful.

As for me, I had a great time at Nottingham, but if I'd remained in the field of electrical and electronic engineering there probably would have been a nuclear disaster by now. When I graduated, the opportunity to change the world never fell into my lap so I decided to do a master's in information technology. I came through it, but I must confess I'm still not very good with computers and am more than capable, with a single keystroke, of crashing most pieces of IT I come into contact with.

Fed up and unwanted by employers, I then headed to Cornwall to change direction. I fancied myself as a writer and Redruth College was running a sixteen-week journalism accreditation course. Most importantly, it was the cheapest of its kind around. Having missed out on several BBC journalism trainee courses around the country – and one for the newspaper industry run by *The Observer* – this was my last throw of the dice before … well, I simply don't know.

Three days after arriving in Redruth, I was summoned to Basing-stoke. I'd almost forgotten about the job I'd applied for there. It was advertised in a left-wing newspaper called *Tribune*: the Basingstoke

Labour Party was looking for a part-time agent/administrator and was prepared to pay £6,000 a year to the lucky candidate. My Ford Escort wasn't going to be up to the trip from Cornwall – it had only just managed to get me there from west London, groaning every mile of the way – so I got the train and a cab to the Basingstoke Labour club, which, due to bad weather, took about six hours. It's a good thing I had left early: it afforded me the time to pop into the local library to read up on Basingstoke politics.

I was later to learn that I was there to make up the numbers and the job had already been lined up for someone else. But, as I looked them in the eye at the Labour club that night, perhaps somebody looked down on me and gave me a break. At long last.

Councillors Angela Wells and Colin Reagan were on the selection committee, but the main man was an elderly, boisterous fella by the name of Stan Parry, who took no prisoners. Stan was old school. I'm told he once got into a row with a Labour Party regional officer for using the phrase 'like niggers in a woodpile' at a CLP meeting. Let me tell you, that's incendiary at a Labour Party meeting.

Impressed by the bit of research I'd done on Basingstoke – and perhaps charitable about how hungry I was for this eighteen-hours-a-week job (for which I was prepared to work twenty-hour shifts) – they rang me that night and told me the job was mine if I wanted it. My parents were in India on holiday at the time but my big brother passed on a message to me with which I'm sure they would have concurred: 'What are you doing?! Where?! Why?!'

An entirely understandable response. I'd done a degree in electrical and electronic engineering but didn't stick at it. I'd done a master's in IT but couldn't find anyone to give me a job. I had the skills to be a good journalist but was now walking away from that to be a part-time agent in a political backwater. But it felt right.

I had no patronage. My political journey, if there was to be one, would not have any ladders to haul me up. I'd start from the bottom and do it myself. The hard way. At least I wouldn't be beholden to anyone, apart from the kindness of Angela Wells and the friendship of Colin Reagan in the years ahead. And then there was my new boss – the ball-breaker who was Stan Parry, chair of the Basingstoke Labour Party.

Stan had invented his own campaigning structure involving his home computer, a database of Labour supporters he'd inputted from scratch, his own brand of leaflets (the Winklebury Banners), and a sergeant-major attitude to his Labour ward candidates that led to three Tories being replaced by three Labour councillors.

He drove me mad. He'd ring twenty times a day and shriek the words: 'Organisation, organisation, organisation – that's how we win!' But he taught me so much. Yes, even though he fell out with absolutely everyone – and I mean *everyone*. I was the courier for messages from Stan to the Labour South East regional office, where the conversation would go something like this:

'Parmjit from Basingstoke here.'

'Hi Parmjit. You have a message from Stan?'

'Yes, he told me to tell you: "Arseholes".'

'Thanks, Parmjit. Hope you have a good day.'

'No problem. Speak to you later, I expect.'

When I began working for Stan, he brought in a big book. He wanted me to put in it any days I couldn't work.

'You know,' he said. 'Special days? Holidays and stuff.'

'I don't understand, Stan.'

'You know, like Christmas or Rub-a-dub.'

'Ah, I think you mean Ramadan, Stan. But I'm not actually a Muslim.'

As well as teaching me how to deal with a tough employer, Stan taught me a lot about how to be meticulous when it comes to campaigning – and life generally. The other thing I learnt – and you may well disagree with me on it – is this: people sometimes say inappropriate things and, although it's easy to be unforgiving, we're all prisoners of our own upbringing, age, times and people around us.

One day, just over five years after starting work in Basingstoke, I would represent a white, working-class city in the west of England. I'd meet many people there who would inadvertently say inappropriate things, but not out of malice. You know when someone has hatred in their soul, but many people I've met just haven't encountered someone like me before and they're finding their way.

Without Stan, Angela and Colin it would never have happened for me. My stuttering start was over. My time in Basingstoke would be finished in just five months. A much bigger role was on its way come June 1996 – with the 1997 general election around the corner – and my progress was about to become exponential.

Three people saw something in me that nobody else had – or they'd just taken pity on me. Either way, I'll always be grateful.

CHAPTER 6

THE NEXT CHAPTER

I WAS TWENTY-FOUR YEARS old. It was 8 June 1996. The opening day of Euro '96 at Wembley Stadium and I was about to sit down in front of the TV to watch England toil to a 1–1 draw against Switzerland.

The phone rang and I leapt up before my mum or dad could get to it because I sensed this one might be for me. Over the years I would get used to the slow, thoughtful London drawl at the other end of the phone. It oozed a quiet authority I would often try to ape but rarely got right.

'This is Terry Ashton, general secretary of the London Labour Party.'

My mind was a whirl. *Do small talk, but don't say anything stupid!* So I said very little, other than it had been nice to meet him and the huge selection committee that morning at Ruskin Hall in Acton. Terry apologised for the size of the interview committee, but alluded to politics and the need to have all eight or so people there, sat in a makeshift U shape, to 'manage the local politics of the West London Agency'. Looking back, the U shape was probably to make it harder for them to kick each other under the table.

I thought my presentation – with OHP slides about SMART goals and how I had helped to change the world in sixteen weeks in Basingstoke – had gone pretty smoothly. I even included a schematic that suggested May's local election results were set to lead to a Labour parliamentary gain there on general election day.

And then Terry said something that I found quite interesting. 'Not sure how you slipped under our radar until now.' It's amazing – for a tall, lanky Asian, I seemed to find myself regularly slipping under the radars of potential employers.

As I dried up on things to say – and was about to come up with something stupid about whether he thought Gazza should be playing this afternoon (or something equally irrelevant) – Terry asked me when I could start the role: £17,500 per year plus pension as west London Labour Party organiser. The contract was funded part locally, part nationally, so they had licence to use my skills wherever necessary – whatever it took to win the 1997 general election and make Tony Blair the first Labour Prime Minister in eighteen years.

Terry felt I was the right man for this job in particular. It was, after all, my manor – I understood the local cultures and he had the foresight to realise I was a good match for what they needed. I wasn't going to turn it down.

By the time England were being knocked out on penalties by the Germans in the semi-final, I was saying my final goodbyes to the Basingstoke General Management Committee. Yes, Stan Parry had made all thirty members of the committee turn up for the regular monthly meeting, regardless of our protests about the football being on.

We got through business quite quickly that night. Down in the bar I had a few pints with Colin Reagan – who would become a friend for life – but not before Stan took me aside for some words of wisdom. 'I'll be keeping an eye on you,' he said. 'Do you think you might come back one day and be a parliamentary candidate in Basingstoke?'

That was high praise indeed, and because it was coming from Stan it meant that much more to me. In a few short weeks he'd raised my sights in life. Being a candidate for somewhere like Basingstoke was way above the summit of my expectations in 1996.

But the next two years would change my life forever. Ruskin Hall in Acton – my office and home from home between 1996 and 1998 – was just a shortish drive through heavy traffic from Hayes each day down the Uxbridge Road. It was also a journey down memory lane through Southall Broadway: past the house my parents rented a room in and subsequently bought when they saved enough after arriving from Punjab; past the shops where Mum had dragged us out shopping every Saturday morning as kids; past our local Sikh temples and the samosa-laden restaurants that … well, that we never actually visited because Mum would say it was better to eat the ones she made at home – and save money – although they still looked and smelt nice.

The journey snaked through Ealing, past the town hall, cinema and shops, and into Acton to Ruskin Hall – under the shadow of the giant South Acton Estate.

Although this was the part of the world I grew up in, I had to immerse myself in a different kind of history to understand my new assignment.

My local priorities were broadly summed up as follows…

There were four local parliamentary constituencies in the patch: Ealing Southall; Ealing North; Ealing, Acton & Shepherd's Bush; and, finally, Hammersmith & Fulham. Ealing Southall was a safe Labour seat with a diminutive MP called Piara Khabra – the first Sikh Member of Parliament. Ironically, I am now the last surviving Labour Sikh to have served in Parliament. Khabra was paranoid about losing his seat, despite the fact he would become leader of the Labour Party if Labour fell back to just one seat in the House, because it would probably be his seat. Those would be the only circumstances in which Piara would become Labour leader, though. He was a former member of the Communist Party, the Labour Party, the SDP and then, of course, the Labour Party once more. I found a typo in his 1997 general election address quite amusing. He wrote: 'I'm a democratic soloist.' I'm assuming he meant socialist.

Although small in size, he was a political giant in Southall – loved, feared and loathed in equal measures. I never quite understood why people feared him until I got to know and understand him and the history of local politics in Southall. His unwritten history tells a tale in itself and is a marker of how politics from the Indian subcontinent would continue to challenge and confuse the Labour Party hierarchy to the modern day. But I'll return to this theme later.

My job was to keep Piara calm, keep him out of the news and keep him out of trouble (my success, alas, was limited here) since the new Labour machine fixated on winning its key seats and shutting down all distractions. Piara's members should have been campaigning in the neighbouring key seat of Brentford & Isleworth – which we were trying to gain – but that was not on his agenda.

The constituency was rife with medieval-style feuding due to balkanised membership blocks held by half a dozen membership barons. The average CLP has between 300 and 400 members; Southall had 5,000 at its peak. Something was always simmering.

So, with Labour's biggest moment looming in 1997, one of my greatest roles would be to contain and control the feuding in Ealing Southall.

Ealing North was a whole different kettle of fish. I was to give special attention to Steve Pound in Ealing North. Steve was (and is) beguilingly streetwise and sharp – in many ways, better equipped for stand-up comedy than public life. He scared the hell out of the Labour high command because they never understood whether he was being serious or just fooling around. I've never asked him if it's true or not, but I'm told at one time he had most of the Parliamentary Labour Party believing that a former Labour minister had been a belly-dancer prior to taking up her seat. He was well known and well loved among the voters, with a tale to tell about most of them – and they had some great yarns about him too.

His seat was not considered a key seat by a party obsessed with 'Operation Victory' – the strategy that said we would target all of our efforts in ninety key seats and no others. Tory Harry Greenway had been the local MP since 1979 and had a majority of over 8,000. But I knew the demographics were changing: the Asian vote was on the move in Ealing and Steve was set to gain from it. Steve was as brilliant with people as he was madcap and unpredictable. He was the perfect opponent for Harry Greenway and, whatever the party said, I was determined to fight this seat like a key seat because I knew Steve could win it. In any case, it was going to be a real roller-coaster ride working with him so I was ready to burn the midnight oil to help make it happen.

Ealing, Acton & Shepherd's Bush was a new seat combining Labour MP Clive Soley's Shepherd's Bush with Tory Sir George Young's Ealing Acton. As I had swapped Hampshire for west London, Sir George did a bunk and headed the other way on the chicken-run to the safe seat of North West Hampshire.

Clive Soley was the chair of the Parliamentary Labour Party, a delight to work with and completely sensible. We were going to win the seat and he knew it. The local party was pragmatic and low maintenance, which made everyone's life easier – including mine.

Hammersmith & Fulham had its own organiser and a group of people running the show who never wanted to have anything to do with my end of west London. It was a bit bizarre, but you know when sometimes people look at you and just don't like the cut of your jib. Well, one or two folk down at the Hammersmith end seemed to want to throw acid on my suit before even meeting me.

In summary, my duties were: hold Ealing, Acton & Shepherd's

Bush; don't let Southall descend into a bloodbath; gain Ealing North; and pull the Hammersmith knives out of my back at every opportunity.

Welcome to London politics and the biggest learning curve of my life.

CHAPTER 7

THE WILD WEST

HE INTERNAL WARS of the mass membership of Ealing Southall had been calmed. As long as the legal paperwork had been completed for the candidate – which I made sure it had been – all was OK there.

Ealing, Acton & Shepherd's Bush was a new seat, but it already had a decent majority on paper. The local party was focused and needed no extra support. Indeed, they were looking to assist neighbouring seats to see if they could help deliver a landslide. Ealing North was my baby. I had nurtured it, calmed troubled waters, recruited new members and helped retrain the existing ones to form what had become a formidable election-fighting machine with a hungry and committed candidate at its helm.

I look back at the detail of my planning for polling day – and at the weeks, even months, of work in the run-up to it – and realise I must have been a rather obsessive and demented man. But this was once-in-a-lifetime stuff. I had my memories of the 1979, 1983, 1987 and 1992 general election defeats and I had only ever really known a life under a Tory government.

With six weeks to polling day, John Major had prorogued parliament, kicking off the longest election campaign in history.

Within twenty-four hours of Major's announcement, I received an unexpected phone call from John Braggins, one of the senior campaign co-ordinators in Millbank Tower. John is a good guy with more election campaigning experience than anyone I know. He's also one of the few white people to have overseen a mass meeting in one of the Southall Labour Party wards. He had the good sense to withdraw to the pub when somebody drew a ceremonial sword at him during the meeting. Sometimes knowing when to retreat is a gift too.

But John wasn't ringing to chew the cud on campaigns of yesteryear. The organiser for the Swindon North seat had effectively received a knife between the shoulder blades from the local party. She had been relieved of her responsibilities, thus leaving a slightly panicked Millbank with a key seat lacking a full-timer to report on every heartbeat. This was a seat that had to be kept out of the news.

The candidate was Michael Wills (now Lord Wills). Gordon Brown had introduced him to the constituency party and was one of his closest buddies. North and South Swindon were new constituencies; in 1992 they were just a single seat, which Labour lost by only a few hundred votes. The incumbent candidate was Jim De Avila, an official for what is now the powerful Unite union. In the ensuing power struggle, the Brownite Michael Wills beat De Avila in the selection for North Swindon. This set off months of arguments about whether the ballot had been fair or if it had been manipulated in some way by the party to get the local union man out and get the well-heeled and well-connected former owner of Juniper Productions in. The Swindon Labour Party had become poisonous. In-fighting and backbiting was the order of the day.

I know people who worked for the party nationally at the time who were convinced that the sealed ballot boxes that lay in the cellar of a Labour Party office somewhere might show a different result to the one that was declared at the selection. But we'll never know – and frankly that wasn't my problem (although, in a way, it was about to be). John Braggins was ringing to ask me to forsake my duties in west London, including what Millbank had decreed to be a 'non-key seat' in Ealing North, and go to Swindon for the remainder of the campaign.

As you can imagine, this was difficult for me. I was flattered: I'd moved from Basingstoke to west London because I was ambitious, and now the hierarchy was offering me one of its coveted key seats to manage. But I'd also invested so much of myself in building up the Ealing North Labour Party and I was weeks away from seeing it through to something special.

When I shared my dilemma with the officers of Ealing and Steve Pound, they went ape. Not with me, but with Millbank. Steve was really down. 'I feel as if my balls have been cut off,' he said. Not sure what that made me, but I took it as a compliment.

So I did a deal. It was six weeks to polling day and I could do it all. Millbank and Ealing agreed that I would work seven days a week (no additional pay obviously, but I was running on adrenalin by then). I'd cover the two Swindon seats (including a watching brief for the non-key seat of Swindon South) as well as my west London responsibilities over a four-day and three-day split week. And every day would be a long day.

Swindon, which was being treated like a school in special measures, was not informed of the plan. They thought they'd got rid of their organiser, were free from Millbank interference and could now run their own campaign – so we were on a serious collision course.

When I first set foot in Swindon I went straight to the election HQ – the Pinehurst People's Centre. A crowd of around thirty local activists were milling around, having one of their regular mêlées in the committee room. It was a meeting-cum-gossip time/envelope-stuffing session with a lot of hot air and little activity. Don't get me wrong, there were a lot of good people there, but the election machine was dysfunctional due to the personality clashes and feuding at the top of the party. Instead of being indoors arguing, they needed to be outdoors meeting the electorate.

And what did they make of me? Walking into the giant room at Pinehurst was like that scene from the film *Blazing Saddles* when the black sheriff walks into the bar and everything goes silent. I could feel the antagonism towards me. Does this kid from London expect to waltz in here and tell us how to run our election campaign? I even received an aggressive phone call from a self-appointed election co-ordinator who made a really coarse attempt to intimidate me, hoping I'd turn on my heels and go scurrying back to London. It wasn't going to happen; I grew up in a rougher environment than most people I know in politics.

I also had a trump card, so they couldn't touch me: I had been appointed to do the job and I answered to the party nationally, not locally. Plus the whole thing was set to be over in six weeks in any case, so why should I care about stamping on a few eggshells if it got a few difficult souls out of the election centre and a few more votes for Labour in the ballot box? My job was to keep things going as smoothly as possible, make sure the in-fighting stayed out of the news and report on the canvassing returns to the regional office.

Michael Wills is a very intelligent man and very likeable when you get to know him, but I would not really get to know him until I became a colleague of his in Parliament. However, in these circumstances, when my sole purpose in life was to get more juice out of what you call 'candidates' (and we organisers called 'legal necessities'), we were bound to clash. And we did. I hope he doesn't hold it against me, but I was just doing my job. Michael was everything I'll never be in the Labour Party – very well heeled, very well connected and very intelligent. Probably why he's now an ex-MP who is in the House of Lords and I'm an ex-MP who is not. He was also very frustrating when I needed him to be in Swindon, rather than London, doing key campaigner visits and, most importantly, meeting voters.

The 1997 New Labour play book was all about beasting your candidates to death on the doorstep, the theory being that if a voter meets a candidate they are five times more likely to vote for them. Steve Pound in Ealing North couldn't get enough of meeting people on the doorstep – to the point where we'd have to drag him away – so perhaps I was unfair when I split my time between Ealing North and Swindon to be setting my targets at Ealing North levels of activity.

On the last Saturday before polling day, much to the annoyance of Labour Party activists around the country, the leadership pushed the envelope by amending the party colours from red to purple and red. I'm afraid this appealed to my darker side, for which I hope Swindon activists will forgive me. After much lobbying I got Michael and his team to agree to stand outside the home end of Swindon Town Football Club's final game of the season to hand out leaflets. They were dressed in full purple and red livery. Years later, at a party conference, I was asked by a Swindon activist if I was aware who the visiting team was that day and what their team colours were. Yes, I did know it was Crystal Palace – and I knew they wore purple and red. It's time I apologised. I'm sorry.

Kind of.

CHAPTER 8

1 MAY 1997 – A NEW DAWN

BY THE TIME I arrived at Greenford Hall for the Ealing North count I'd been up for twenty hours – but the adrenalin was pumping and I'd never felt so alive. Regardless of the local argy-bargy, when I left Swindon North at about 5 p.m., I felt certain we were going to win it. I had a good feeling we would take the non-key seat of Swindon South too. The Southall and Ealing, Acton & Shepherd's Bush seats were also already in the bag.

But I was a bit irate that, after months of detailed planning, something had gone wrong in one of the Ealing North wards. The person I had trained to run the operation there had been pushed aside by a bolshy local councillor who didn't understand the systems or what he was meant to be doing. I hadn't the time to be arguing and made this tricky situation my first port of call. I went into the councillor's house, took the squalid mash of what should have been knock-up sheets organised into street groups and divvied them up to the glum-looking activists.

I was the agent and they knew I'd had a long day. They also knew what had been expected of them, although this wasn't the time for a post-mortem or a debate about whether it would lead to a narrow defeat.

But I still had that Hayes & Harlington defeat by fifty-three votes in my head, so I smiled, told them it was time to recover the situation – get out there and knock on the doors we had data for – and watched the local councillor disappear into a darkened room for the rest of the night.

As the sun shone into the late evening, the feedback from the wards was all OK. It was time. It was going to be *our* time.

. . .

I rang Terry Ashton. He was my big boss and he needed to know. It was around 3 a.m. on Friday 2 May 1997.

I was going to finish this off as calmly and professionally as I possibly could. I was put through to Terry and the conversation went something like this:

'So you finished off the job in Swindon and made it back to Ealing?'

'Yes, all done. Haven't heard any news of declarations in Swindon but I'm pretty sure we'll take Swindon North and Swindon South too. I spoke to the RD [regional director] earlier.'

'Well done. So what news of Ealing North?'

'We're just about to declare here at Greenford Hall, Terry.'

I wanted to savour this moment. It was like having the co-ordinates for the gold buried at the end of the rainbow. Only I, the agent, the returning officer and the candidates had this precious piece of information. And I knew my history. Never had a party achieved a 6 per cent swing before to win a general election. My project in Ealing North was to achieve a swing of 8 per cent to overturn a majority of 6,000.

'Terry, we've overturned their 6,000 majority and won by over 9,000. I make it around a 16 per cent swing, Tory to Labour.'

There was a long pause from the Greater London Labour Party regional office. I had taken up a quiet spot behind a pillar at Greenford Hall. The public gallery looking down on us was packed with our activists. My dad and brother had come down to give me moral support. On the floor of Greenford Hall, the assortment of rosettes of all the main parties was on display. I'd made sure my counting agents were well drilled and had kept their focus on the trestle tables in front of them, looking out for every single spoilt ballot paper. Their focus and their discipline had been immense.

They were tuned into their radios. They were becoming increasingly aware this was going to be an extraordinary night. Their eyes were on Steve Pound. They were also looking at me to tell them how it was going.

Terry spoke at last: 'So, the Parliamentary Labour Party is going to have to put up with Steve Pound as an MP then.'

He made me laugh. I think he was joking but could never be certain, so simply said: 'I think they'll cope!'

'Well done,' Terry added. 'But make sure he's behaving himself. What's he up to?'

I looked across the hall. Steve Pound was standing on a chair and conducting a sing-song in the gallery above him to the tune of Baddiel & Skinner's 'Three Lions'. He was singing at the top of his voice: 'He's on the dole, he's on the dole ... Portillo's on the dole!'

I covered the mouthpiece of my phone and moved out to the corridor. 'He's fine, Terry. A bit quiet, probably overcome by the occasion...'

．　．　．

It should have been time to let up a little, but I couldn't. The returning officer called the candidates and agents into a huddle to discuss spoilt ballot papers. Steve Pound was ready to do handstands by then and begin his lap of honour – and he would have been right to celebrate: the pile of votes we had built up was dwarfing everything else on the table. It wasn't close.

But the Tory MP Harry Greenway wanted to squabble over each and every one of the forty spoilt ballot papers. At one point he was hopping up and down saying: 'That one's got my name on it, my name is on it! It's mine.'

The returning officer turned to me to see if I'd let him have it. I quietly reminded him, the candidates and the other agents that, according to electoral law, if someone has written a name on a ballot paper then technically it can't be counted because of the possibility the voter is being identified in what is a secret ballot. Harry persisted: 'It's got my name on it!'

Unfortunately for him, the returning officer had to side with me and, in any case, when you write the words 'Harry Greenway is a twat' on a ballot paper, it can't be counted as valid.

This went on for about ten minutes until eventually I looked at the little envelope of spoilt papers – and the mountain of Labour votes dwarfing the Tory and Lib Dem piles – I pointed to the spoilt papers and said, 'Harry, just take the bloody lot,' or something similar. He marched off.

He was soon comforted by Steve's acceptance speech, in which Steve said: 'I'm sure John Major will show Harry Greenway exactly the esteem he holds him in come the next honours list.' It wasn't a compliment, but Harry didn't realise and smiled at the thought.

Steve also said something else in his speech that I'll always remember. He thanked everyone for the efforts they put into getting him elected and then he added that, although the local Labour Party *wanted* to win that night, Parmjit Dhanda *had* to win that night. Looking back, he was right.

The returning officer announced that the Tory majority of just under 6,000 had now become a Labour majority of 9,160. A swing of 16.1 per cent.

Job done.

CHAPTER 9

THE TROT OF STOKE ROCHFORD HALL

I N THE LATE 1990s, Labour Party apparatchiks invented a new swear word. If you didn't fit the image of New Labour – modern, business-like and 100 per cent on-message – then you could be labelled a 'Trot'. Doesn't sound too bad, does it?

I think most apparatchiks who used the phrase Trot assumed it meant 'left-wing trouble-maker'. But Trot is actually short for Trotskyite – a supporter of Leon Trotsky.

Trotsky joined the Russian Bolsheviks prior to the 1917 October

Revolution. He served as the People's Commissar for Foreign Affairs in the Soviet Union before founding and then commanding the Red Army. Among other things, he was a leading light in the Politburo.

To be honest with you, I didn't know most of this stuff prior to researching this book, which would make me a pretty poor-quality follower of Trotsky – although not in the minds of some of my then colleagues, I was to learn.

Trotsky was something of a left-wing ideologue. He stood up to Soviet leader Joseph Stalin until he and his family were hunted down and killed in Mexico. There was no hiding place from Stalin. Trotsky was found dead with an ice-pick in his head in 1940. I was not involved in any of these events and can assure followers of both Stalin and Trotsky that I'd much rather stay out of such altercations. Ice-picks are not my thing.

Trot was one of the worst labels you could be given in Labour circles in the 1990s. It had nothing to do with Trotsky – if it did, what did that make the people who used the phrase? As enemies of Trotskyites, I guess they would have to be Stalinists. Trot became a safe insult to use to exclude or blacklist people who were different, unwanted or left-wingers at a time when the rightward move of New Labour was in the ascendency.

Despite the fact that I was a member of party staff myself, I'd attracted enemies from somewhere – people were whispering about me. At first I tried to laugh it off, but sometimes you can sense when you walk into a room and people are looking at you a bit differently or you just know the topic of conversation has changed due to your presence. My worry was that if you give a dog a bad name, the name sticks. And I was young. I didn't really fancy an ice-pick in my head.

Perhaps when I was new to my career as a member of party staff, I let my guard down a bit among colleagues (would-be friends?) and played up to being a bit left due to my upbringing. I had a chip on my shoulder about being one of the few working-class people in an intellectually middle-class environment – and I still do. I was learning how to interact with these people and that put me outside of my comfort zone. That didn't make me a Marxist revolutionary, but it must have presented an opportunity for people who didn't think I was the right kind of person to be helping to shape the Labour Party.

Terry Ashton and his deputy had both warned me that rumours of my 'left-wing past' were being put around – that I was a confidant of left-wing MP Alan Simpson; that I used to sell the *Socialist Worker*. Alan was my MP at Nottingham University and seemed like a nice guy, but I never actually even had a conversation with him until after we both become colleagues in Parliament – some years later. Thoroughly nice bloke, I should add, but we never plotted a revolution together.

The only thing I was guilty of was naivety. And being tall, young, gangly and with a brown skin made me much more visible. These were attributes that would help me at times and hold me back at others. I hadn't studied politics at university, A level or even GCSE. I hadn't ever sold the *Socialist Worker* – I didn't know what it was. I knew nothing of Trotsky, the Tolpuddle Martyrs or the Jarrow marchers. My knowledge and experience was contemporary: Thatcher; the failure of our public services; the miners' strike; the Southall riots; in-your-face racism…

My experience was real, even though I was working class and

born into intellectual poverty compared with those around me and those circling above me. I had never anticipated a political career, so I was, in many senses, a fish out of water.

Through a combination of good fortune and help from people who knew me best in the party, I managed to dodge some ice-picks. Looking back now at the age of forty-three, I now know how lucky I was to ever have a political career at all. It was a bit like being Indiana Jones in the *Last Crusade*. You know the bit at the end where he's set three impossible challenges to reach the Holy Grail? I ended up ducking under those circular discs with the serrated edges, rolling over and jumping to avoid the next one without ever really knowing what was to come at me next or from which direction. I know others more talented than I who were not so lucky trying to guess how to spell Jehovah in ancient Latin.

But it's also amazing how quickly things can change. When I was on top in politics, when I'd made it, the world was with me. But when you're an underdog on your way up (or down), you're pretty much on your own.

After I was selected as Labour's PPC for Gloucester in 2000 I became a darling of the party. I was one of just three new ethnic minority candidates who had been selected in winnable seats. The party encouraged Rosalba O'Brien of *The Observer* to spend a day campaigning with me a week before the 2001 general election. She wrote: 'Dhanda is everything you would expect of New Labour – slick, professional, with the common touch.'

I wonder what Trotsky would have made of that.

So I went from being a left-wing lunatic in 1998 to the embodi-ment of New Labour by 2001. Of course, neither of these things was true – but this episode taught me something about the dangers of the political village. If you're 'different', you stand out.

As I was to learn at Stoke Rochford Hall in 1998…

. . .

The big moment, and the big threat for me, came in 1998. The Labour Party was to select its candidates for the 1999 European elections under a new system. It involved regional lists of candidates instead of constituencies. One of the reasons for the changes given at the time was to make our MEPs more 'representative' of society. It was also a blunt tool for the party to get rid of a swathe of sitting MEPs who it felt were rather too independent-minded.

My personal standing in Ealing was as high as it could be in the local Labour Party: I had delivered in 1997; I had overseen the re-election of Ealing Council with an increased Labour majority in 1998; and now, aged nearly twenty-seven, I had been elected on to Hillingdon Council (the neighbouring authority to Ealing). It was time to take a risk.

I decided to write to the three parties in Ealing, their councillors and their MPs to say I'd be standing down as the borough's Labour Party organiser. I was genuinely grateful for their support, but it was time to move on. I'd achieved all I could have wanted there and it was time to cash in my chips. I had no job lined up to go to.

I never wanted to be an MEP, but people had been tapping me on the shoulder locally after seeing me in action. I was becoming a decent orator; I had the ability to stand in front of hordes of party members, who had been press-ganged into attending local councillor selection meetings on behalf of the people who had paid their membership, and I could reason with them with authority and in more than one language. My parents and grandparents were entrenched in the local Sikh community and I was becoming well known, well regarded and entrenched in the local Labour Party. The local overlaps were strong.

There was, and still is, a major issue of under-representation of ethnic minorities in Parliament. I'd shown my mettle as a campaigner and, crucially, having met the party's talents, I no longer felt intimidated. My ambition was starting to burn. The 1999 Euro elections (if I were to be a candidate) could be my chance to learn, grow and catapult myself into a political career.

A few weeks after I handed in my notice to the Ealing parties, the complex process to choose Labour's Euro candidates began. So I got my first experience of hustings meetings – debates against other candidates in front of Labour Party activists as they vote for their candidates. I focused my energies on two areas: North West Hampshire (after my Basingstoke experience) and west London. In Basingstoke I won the hustings meeting I took part in, which guaranteed me a place on a ballot paper within the Labour Party's selection process.

Party members in each Euro constituency would then vote for a man and a woman to put through to the final stage – an assessment board at Stoke Rochford Hall in Lincolnshire. Stalin would have been proud of this process: start with democracy involving the members and then override it with an assessment centre of the great and the good. But there was no point in me worrying about that; I still had to reach first base.

During a frantic week I attended a further six hustings meetings in front of west London audiences in the constituencies of: Twickenham; Hammersmith & Fulham; Ealing, Acton & Shepherd's Bush; Feltham & Heston; Brentford & Isleworth; Ealing Southall; and Ealing North.

My pitch was partly local (*I'm just a local lad, born down the road*), partly personal (*Look at what I've done for you over the last two years!*) and partly organisational (*You know I can run a campaign*). Every single local party nominated me. I won all six. This politics lark was a cinch!

Michael Cashman, an actor from *EastEnders* who was adored by the party leadership (and was destined to do well), swept up most of the London nominations. But I had won west London with a clean sweep, and was thereby through to the assessment board stage, no ballot required. Neena Gill (now a West Midlands MEP) prevailed in the women's half of the draw in many parts of London. Local councillor Pam Wharfe, whom I'd got to know quite well, was the successful woman in west London.

At last I had the opportunity I'd been yearning for: to stand for the Labour Party in a national election and see if I had what it took to cut the mustard. Victory in all of those hustings meetings had made me a much more confident and polished young performer. I wanted to show my party what I could do for it; how I could help make the world a better place. So I was off to Stoke Rochford Hall, the stately home owned by the National Union of Teachers, to meet the party bigwigs.

Thankfully I was too naive to know that this was where the fun and games were really about to play out. And where the ice-picks were being sharpened.

. . .

Puking up in a toilet basin a couple of hours before being grilled by the selection board was not great preparation. The rooms at Stoke Rochford Hall are sumptuous and as fine as any quality hotel you'll find. But Lincolnshire seemed a long way from home. The large comfortable room felt like a prison cell for me that night as I paced around my room. I'd convinced myself that my ten-minute presentation on 'Why Europe Matters to Us' was total crap. So I started re-writing it for the umpteenth time. By 4 a.m. I decided to just go back to bed. But then I was worried that one of my alarm clocks (yes, I had two just in case) wouldn't work and I'd sleep through my big moment. Fat chance of that!

So I woke up tired and full of nerves. As I got into my suit I couldn't help but be violently sick. Thankfully I didn't get any of it on the suit. The rooms in the accommodation block were full of seasoned campaigners and experienced MEPs. I remember looking in the bathroom mirror and giving myself a good shake. 'What have you got to lose? Nothing. Nothing.' I'd half-filled the basin with water from the cold tap before climbing into bed and had left a can of Stella Artois in it, just in case, to settle my nerves.

A night without sleep, a body overcome by nerves and a head discombobulated by a speech I didn't trust any more were rounded off with a can of strong beer on an empty stomach. It strangely revived me and I was ready to take on the biggest day of my political life. Perhaps the most important day I would ever have. Failure would end my dreams before they had even begun.

Stoke Rochford Hall is a trade union building but it's also one of the most beautiful stately homes you can imagine. It wasn't exactly the kind of place that put me in my comfort zone. I found a quiet corner on a plush sofa in the giant high-ceilinged lounge and waited to do my presentation. Scores of would-be MPs wandered around making chit-chat. After all it had taken to get this far, everything now hung on a ten-minute presentation. Following that, many of us would be sent home. The reward for the survivors would be a grilling from the selection board in the afternoon and that process would supposedly decide the order of Labour's lists.

Looking back, we all now know that the top of most of the orders of the Euro lists had already been stitched up or would be stitched up by trade union officials, members of regional boards and senior party staff during the course of the afternoon. The presentations and Q&As were largely inconsequential. But, for a 26-year-old rather unknown quantity like myself, I had a place on a list to play for – or, equally, I could be sent home if I was not up to par.

'Parmjit Dhanda, will you come through, please.' My turn in the grand boardroom. Stony faces behind a giant U-shaped table in front of me – about twenty of them. Ian McCartney MP was at the opposite end of the table. Ian was a firebrand trade unionist MP – well regarded and truly fierce. Not a flicker of a smile. I had met him once or twice at by-elections when I worked for the party, but I doubted he would remember me. There were some senior party staff members there who I knew, including Terry – tucked away at the back to my right – and David Gardner – the assistant general secretary of the Labour Party – who was running the show.

I didn't recognise most of the others – a mixture of party members who held officer roles in the regions and some trade union heavies, interspersed among party staff.

Sixteen years down the line, the speech I made is something of a blur. Probably just as well. It was a mixture of the need to make Europe more relevant to the people of Britain and the need to have the youth, energy and vigour to campaign for every vote. It wasn't bad at all, although it certainly wasn't Kennedy or Obama either. Other than the flicker of a smile from Terry, I was a bit perturbed by the stony faces around the room. But I left feeling I'd had a good shot at it and hadn't let myself down. I just desperately wanted to come back for the combat of the 'hostile interview' in the afternoon.

It was a brutal day. I sat in the giant lounge talking to Pam Wharfe, the councillor from Hounslow, as dozens of frazzled candidates climbed the walls waiting to hear their fate. But Pam made me laugh. If I'd had a difficult night it was nothing compared to hers. Her young daughter had got into a strop about her mother going away for the night and hence she'd set off for Lincolnshire really late. She got lost driving up in the dark and had ended up sleeping in her car in a lay-by, only just finding the venue in time to get her suit and make-up on in time to deliver her speech.

And then, very suddenly, it happened. A group of young staffers walked among us, armed with a list. They tapped people on the shoulder and whispered, 'Thanks but you can go home now, I'm sorry,' or, 'Well done, they'd like you to stay for the afternoon session.'

I remember the hollow look in the eyes of people who were

being sent home. Some were angry but holding it in. Most of all I remember that lost look when you don't know what to do or where to go, tinged with the humiliation of it all being so public. Years later, when I lost my seat in 2010, I would go through those emotions myself at the count on election night and again in Parliament as I cleared out my office in the requisite twenty-four hours before they lock you out. And on both occasions, after seeing colleagues go through it in 1998 at Stoke Rochford Hall, I made sure nobody would see that hollow, lost look in my eyes. I never cried or crumbled outside of my own home.

I felt the tap on my shoulder and a lady said, 'You're OK,' before giving me a slot for my afternoon interview. The sense of relief, tinged with guilt for the fallen, left me quite mixed up for a minute. Then I saw Pam – she came over to check on me and I did likewise. We were both OK and we hugged each other. I felt so happy. I went out for some air. Nothing was going to hold me back now. I just wanted to get straight back into the boardroom and tear it up with them. The difficult bit was behind me; after all those months of networking and hustings I would make it to the end of the process. Even if I failed at the final hurdle, I'd proved something to myself.

But my heart really goes out to the people who were victims of the process that day. I know, because I've been told by people who were on that selection panel – and who I've got to know well over the years – that some of the folk who got through the process didn't deserve to and some of those who were cleared out had just picked up enemies or a bad rep. I didn't realise, even at this stage, how close I would come to being one of the victims.

• • •

Round two was back in the boardroom. The twenty hardened faces seemed to have softened, or perhaps they'd just gone stir crazy after a long day in the saddle. Instead of standing to address them, I was invited to take a seat. I took a look around the room and announced: 'I am *not* Munir Malik!'

This had them in fits of laughter. Goodness knows why. Maybe they'd been on the juice over lunch. For my part I was relatively relaxed; having made it this far I felt some of the weight had been lifted from my shoulders. The Munir Malik statement was partially a serious one. Munir was a fellow candidate, albeit a lot older and balder than me and from the other end of London. He was meant to be getting his grilling but had decided to go for a drive with his wife and hadn't made it back. Whether he'd had enough or got lost in Lincolnshire I didn't know, but I had accepted the invitation to step in and take my turn instead. I'm sure all the panel members would have been briefed that I was Parmjit Dhanda, but, in an exclusively white room (apart from me), I just wanted to gently ensure there would be no confusion. I guess I could have just said: 'Look, whitey, I know we all look the same to you, but I'm the other one. OK?' Might not have gone down so well...

There was a plastic cup of water on the table; I picked it up to take a sip and then asked, 'I'm assuming this is potable?' – to which I got an alarmed official rushing towards me with her hand over her mouth. Apparently they'd forgotten to change the water after the last candidate had slurped from the cup. No big deal. I just said something like, 'Well, we're all part of the same Labour family.' And they all fell about laughing again. Perhaps the process was getting to them more than it was to me.

Then it was a case of *ding-ding* and we went straight into battle. The 'hostile interview' involved questions being whizzed in from panel members around the room on a range of topics, never actually involving Europe. It was a bit of a blur, but it felt good. I'd been through so many hustings meetings to get here and had worked for the party for long enough to be able to win battles like this on the domestic agenda without any trouble.

I recall taking the luxury of looking at the clock on the wall after about ten minutes and thinking *so far, so good*. Despite the fact the questions were on domestic policy, I was confident enough to link at least one of the answers to the importance of Europe in our lives.

The session had begun with the taciturn Ian McCartney in the chair, so when the inquisitor role returned to him I knew I was in the final straight. And he really went for me. He does a very good Mr Angry – it's not so much what he says, but the way he uses his shrill Scottish accent and a look of pure venom. 'You, young man, you haven't got a clue! Your policies need to reflect the needs of ordinary working people in this country. People are suffering and politicians like you aren't doing nearly enough to improve the lives of the working classes!' Or words to that effect.

You can go one of two ways in this situation. You can be reasonable and explain that it's not the case – but I felt I had done enough of that in this grilling – or, Plan B, you can fight fire with fire and get shouty – which is what I did. Armed with stats I'd been genning up on for months about poverty and excluded groups, I fired a salvo about women and black people being among the two million people who were about to benefit from a minimum wage under a Labour government. And I didn't need lessons from anyone on poverty and the working class because it was policies like these that benefited people from the community I grew up in and the family I grew up in. There may have been a fist bang on the table too as we glowered at each other across the room. And then there was silence, followed by the hint of a smile from Mr McCartney. Years later, he told me he thought I was polished but he needed to know if I could show passion too – which is why he had turned up the temperature.

Thanks to Ian I'd finished with a bang, bang, bang. Job done. I could have done no more. Only a stitch-up could stop me now.

. . .

So the final deliberations began at Stoke Rochford Hall. Was the party hierarchy going to make me a Labour European parliamentary candidate for the 1999 Euro elections or was it going to end my political career before it had even begun?

When you hear people talking about discussions in smoke-filled rooms, these are the kind of events they are referring to. In the years to come I would hear versions of what went on from Ian McCartney, Terry Ashton and Paul Kenny (who was the London regional secretary of the GMB union and subsequently became the union's general secretary). Over a pint at a Labour Party conference, Paul volunteered that there were people in the room who were out to get me. But he also said that I'd had friends in the room who'd stuck up for me. 'Put a concrete slab on it. Forget it now and move on,' he advised. I found the idea that people had such strong opinions about me really disconcerting, but it was something I had to get used to.

They were out to get me because they saw me as a Trot. My own view is, as I said at the outset of this chapter, that the word Trot was used as a proxy for many things. I listened to Paul and put a slab on it. But I took this to extremes.

I know who tried to shaft me that day and I've never confronted them. I put a concrete slab on it, as the man from the GMB suggested. The person who was really out to get me also used to work with a friend of mine. This friend told me to watch my back as, when stationed outside the office of my secret adversary, he had overheard a conversation about me and – guess what? – the person had referred to me as a Trot and then suggested I shouldn't be allowed to advance to any significant role in the party. This was after Stoke Rochford but before I made it in Gloucester.

There is an irony to this tale, though. When I became an MP, my secret adversary had taken up a very senior role in Labour circles, and, in that role, approached me for a favour. A very big favour. I was asked to help prop up a Prime Minister who was having a very tough time. I thought about it and I obliged, regardless of the attempt to strangle me in my youth, because I had put a slab on it. It's a very Sikh thing to do – or, you might argue, it's a Christian or agnostic thing to do. But I think the whole getting-on-and-grafting thing – and not moaning too much – is quite a Sikh trait.

And it does make me a bit pig-sick of myself. Perhaps there would be more Sikhs in senior positions of public life if we banged our fists harder. Perhaps people like me would have got higher up the ladder if we were prepared to stop being so bloody nice and polite and told people to piss off more often. Alas, it's not our way. I wonder if Trotsky was a secret Sikh.

CHAPTER 10

COMING IN AT
NUMBER FIVE

FOR BYSTANDERS (AND for some of us who were involved)
the 1999 Euro elections must have been something of a
bemusing, even comical event. There were regional lists of
candidates, ranked by their parties in smoke-filled rooms, for an
election to be fought on the bizarre 'D'Hondt' formula of pro-
portional representation in constituencies containing millions of
voters covering large swathes of the country.

The number ones, twos and threes on the regional party lists were either incumbent MEPs who hadn't fallen foul of the party leadership or newcomers who were adored by the party leadership. The bitching between people at the tops of these lists was something to behold. Hardly surprising – particularly if you were the person on the cusp of victory or defeat but felt that candidates who were a shoo-in to win and those who were without a hope of winning were behaving like laggards. In other words, if you were number one on the list, you'd get elected in most regions even if you did no work. If you were number four on the list, you might think you had no chance of victory and hence let the side down with a low work rate. But poor old number two or three knew that they could only win if the party worked really hard, earning those extra seats with everyone pulling their weight. As for the public, they didn't really seem to understand or care for the European elections or the new-fangled system for delivering MEPs.

My former boss Terry Ashton had phoned me to let me know I'd survived the attempt to put an ice-pick through my head and was to be number five on the south-east list of eleven candidates. Three out of the top five were sitting MEPs, another was well regarded by the leadership – and then there was me. This was actually a pretty big shock for me. I'd have been quite thrilled even to scrape in at number eleven. Just being a candidate was all I'd hoped for. Aged twenty-seven at the time, I was the youngest of Labour's Euro candidates in the country and was just a couple of assassinations away from becoming an MEP. That was the rule: if number one and number two on the list fell under a bus, the others would shuffle up the ladder to take their places.

But then something dawned on me. They'd placed me in the

south-east. But the nomination I won, unopposed, was for London. It was fine by me – I'd have happily worked my socks off in the Outer Hebrides if they had asked me – but then I looked up the south-east region and studied the map. My new constituency's northern reaches encompassed Milton Keynes and then stretched south taking in Oxfordshire and Buckinghamshire. Let's not forget Slough and the rest of Berkshire. And Hampshire. It included the Isle of Wight and it curved east to take in the whole of the Sussex coast. It went on and on in a massive doughnut around the M25. Surrey, Kent and goodness knows where else. It was never-ending!

As our lovely regional team of staff and our pool of eleven Euro candidates embarked on their work in 1998 – leafleting; knocking on doors; attending fêtes; visiting Women's Institutes, jumble sales, hustings meetings and you name it – I soon realised that our activity among an electorate of 7.5 million people would feel like throwing a pebble into the ocean with just the faintest hope of causing more than a ripple.

I think the regional staff soon realised the cleverest thing they could do to avoid candidates falling out with each other would be to just get us out knocking on doors in far-flung parts of the world. One Sunday morning in February I was out in deepest Surrey with a small team of candidates and activists enthusiastically knocking on doors to remind people they would soon have the chance to *Vote Labour in the Euro elections! Hurrah!*

A young lady came to the door in her nightgown. It was about 10 a.m. – only politicians would think it bizarre that somebody might still be in bed at that time on a Sunday morning.

'Hi. I'm calling on behalf of the Labour Party. I was just wondering if you'll be voting in the Euro elections on 10 June?'

She looked at me quizzically, wiping the sleep from her eyes. 'Election? There's going to be an election?'

'Yes, the European parliamentary elections. I'm one of the…'

'When?'

'It's not until June 10th but it's really important to let people…'

She raised her hand to put me in pause mode. 'Pal. So there's an election I know nothing about, and I'm not that interested in, which isn't happening for some time yet – yes?'

'Err. Kind of. Do you normally vote Labour?'

'You know, you seem nice. Maybe I will. But it's cold and it's wet. And its Valentine's Day morning. Do you think perhaps people have got other things they might be doing in bed this morning?'

It was a fair point and kind of summed up the campaign. We didn't do well. But I found a niche as the go-to guy on the team who wouldn't say no to any campaigning missions – from hustings on the Isle of Sheppey to Sikh marches through Southampton for Vaisakhi (the festival that marks the creation of the religion). I specialised (as the party expected a loyal puppy like me to) in visiting mandhurs, mosques and gurdwaras from Slough to Gravesend. During that campaign I knocked on doors from Milton Keynes to Portsmouth. I met constituency parties for cupcakes in Faversham and then fundraised in Brighton. I took on other party candidates at a hustings meeting in Oxford University and then went toe-to-toe against the Lib Dem candidate Chris Huhne (remember him?) in leafy Surrey. The last one was at a girls' private school where they weren't even old enough to vote, but I loyally went wherever I was asked to go for the team.

As well as learning about the Labour Party and politics, I also learned a very important lesson about my own culture in 1999. I was on a campaign visit to a gurdwara in Crawley and they asked me to address the congregation, which I did partly in English and partly in Punjabi. As well as making some of the usual political arguments you'd expect about Labour policy – comparing investment under Labour to the bleakness and pain of the Tory years (you know the score) – I wanted to say something more heartfelt about being a boy from their own community. Mum and Dad had joined me on the visit, which encouraged me in my address to the decent-sized *sangat* of around 100 people about what ties us together in our customs from the motherland to the UK. This all feeds into what I feel is a naturally socialist mindset in the Sikh community, even if we don't always acknowledge it. When I finished speaking, it was time for *langar* in the dining hall where I could mingle with my audience and eat chapattis. One well-spoken older gentleman collared me and wanted a political chat. He wore a suit, a bright clean white turban and had a short white beard.

'Young man, that was well said. You speak nicely. I know your neighbourhood well. You are doing a good job. But you didn't talk about the euro today. I want to talk to you about the dangers of the single currency.'

'You know my neighbourhood? Are you from Southall or Hayes?' I asked as I munched on some roti and dahl.

'No, no. I lived there for a while. But this single currency question...'

'Where did you live?'

'Doesn't matter. The problem with the euro…'

'Go on, tell me.'

'I was in Southall before I moved here to Crawley over thirty years ago. Young man, the Labour Party's position on the euro…'

I took a break from munching. 'Which road?'

I sensed a slight exasperation in the way he was now scratching his beard. 'Look, you won't know it. But if you must know it was called Beresford Road. Now let's talk about politics please. The single…'

'What number?'

'Huh? What number what?'

'What number Beresford Road did you live at, Uncle?'

At this point he just shrugged and gave up. 'I lived in Southall for a few months in the 1960s. If you must know, I believe it was number thirty-two. Now let's…'

I put my hand on his shoulder to suggest he should pause for a moment and I called out across the *langar* hall to my dad, who was deep in conversation with either some old or new friends. I beckoned him over and said, 'Dad. This gentleman says he lived on Beresford Road in the 1960s.'

They looked at each other, slightly perplexed. Then Dad spoke. 'Yes. How are you keeping? You didn't have a beard and turban when you lodged with us at 32 Beresford Road.'

They caught up and we never did get to finish that conversation about the euro. But it demonstrates the closeness of the ties within the Asian communities of the UK. You're never far from someone who knows you or a member of your family.

In my own mind, the experience of the 1999 Euro elections had prepared me for what I had to do next. I was becoming a more accomplished and rounded political person and I was ready for a seat in the House of Commons. No more notches on the political bedpost, I decided. *The next selection I fight won't be a dry run; it needs to be for a seat that will get me elected.*

Unfortunately, the Labour Party machine didn't align itself to my political aspirations. They always seemed to have someone else in mind. And that never changed. Sometimes you just have to say: 'Stuff it, I'm going to make it happen anyway.'

CHAPTER 11

GLOUCESTER

THE BACK-END OF 1999 was a difficult time for me. The political adventure seemed to have come to a halt, I was no longer working for the party and the Euro campaign was over. The end of 1999 also saw the end of a long-term relationship with a lovely girl I'd known since university. What can I say about her? She was (and I'm sure still is) warm, attractive, immensely intelligent and one of the loveliest human beings you could ever hope to meet. But we had met rather young and, although the bond between us was strong, it wasn't strong enough to take us from where we were to eternity. So a combination of things had me in a pretty low mood at this time in my life.

I needed the turn of the millennium to provide me with a change in fortune. When this came, it was from an unlikely source – the *Daily Express*. I was having my hair cut in Southall. I would say I was at a hairdresser's or a barber's shop, but I can't really go that far. He was an Asian guy who basically just cut hair. So, rather than trust him with anything complicated, I used to just get him to razor the sides and back as a #1 or #2 and the rest would usually flop into something I could take care of myself (with the help of a bucket of gel or wax). All done for five quid. Those were the days… So, as I sat there asking myself why on earth I hadn't gone to a proper hair stylist, I flicked through yesterday's edition of the *Daily Express*, pausing only to ask the 'haircut man' (trade descriptions won't allow me to call him a barber) to turn down his pulsating bhangra music. The *Express* contained a story about an unhappy MP called Tess Kingham. She was so fed up with the family-unfriendly processes and working hours of Parliament that she was considering standing down. She represented a place called Gloucester.

I had no idea where it was – and, if you'd asked me to locate it on a map, I'd have struggled. As a single man in his mid-to-late twenties, living at home with his parents, I found the thought of spending long hours working in central London and a large chunk of the week away in a constituency actually quite appealing. But, looking around this small room on Southall Broadway known as the 'Clip Place', I had to ask myself whether I was letting my fantasies run away with me. I was about to have a £5 haircut from a man whose own hair was in an unshapely mullet and with a drooping moustache out of the 1970s. The walls were covered in badly cut-out images from magazines of pop stars like Rick Astley and Bollywood actors like Amitabh Bachan. Neither of them, to my knowledge, had ever visited 'Haircut Man' in Clip Place for a cut and blow dry. There were only two other customers in the room. One was an elderly Asian man who had enough hair on his head to cover a marble when he arrived, and looked no different after his haircut. He had decided to remain in the shop, gently rocking in his chair and watching the traffic go by on the Broadway. 'Haircut Man' seemed quite content to let him stay; maybe he was a regular or perhaps this was part of his routine, like a visit to a day centre. Exiting the barber's chair was a teenage Asian lad, who must have been playing truant from school, getting a #1 cut. There was no conversation. He gave his cash and left. My turn. I took my seat as 'Haircut Man' grunted without looking at me – the same as he always did. I went through the ritual of saying what I wanted and he went through the ritual of ignoring me. As usual, he didn't look at me; he just grunted and picked up his electric razor. As long as he didn't use the scissors, I knew I'd be OK. I let him get on with his job and let my mind drift. *Hmm, Gloucester.* It seemed about a million miles from where I was sitting and the world I inhabited.

I thought back to my days as a party organiser when they'd sent me to cover Swindon for the last few weeks of the general election campaign. That experience meant I knew one or two people who worked for the South West Labour Party and apparently Gloucester was in the south-west too. It seemed like something of a pipedream from where I was sitting at that stage in my life. *Perhaps I'll make a call.*

. . .

At that point, my search for a seat had been pretty much stalled in the starting blocks. Labour had a majority of 179, largely made up of new MPs from the 1997 landslide. The only vacancies were going to be among the small number of deaths or retirements. We were not about to start making gains when we already held so many seats – the Labour vote had peaked in 1997 – so competition for the small number of vacancies was immense. Any conversation I had with apparatchiks or union folk would point me in the direction of urban seats because, 'You know, that's where people like you live, isn't it?' But these heartland seats were invariably stitched up for white men from the council with strong local connections or carefully patrolled by big unions for policy wonks who had worked for Cabinet members – who were also invariably white. I had an uncle who was a councillor in West Bromwich, but Tom Watson was nursing that seat. Tom, at that time, was a fixer for what eventually became the Unite trade union and I couldn't afford to put his nose out of joint. I didn't think he would use his influence to support me in other selections, but it wasn't worth having him work actively against me either, so I stayed away from West Bromwich. Wolverhampton South West had a huge Sikh community but not within the local party. The local candidate was a heavily backed guy called Rob Marris who was destined to get the seat. Then there was Birmingham Perry Barr, where I had some backing and was keen to make a go of it. However, I was warned that the membership seemed 'irregular' and was only likely to deliver a Muslim candidate. I wasn't put off and I persisted – only to see the process continually delayed because of these 'irregularities'. I was impatient and couldn't wait for ever, and, in any case, rumours were circulating that the NEC might impose a candidate there.

On the plus side, I'd had a lovely phone call from the Faversham Labour Party in mid Kent. When I attended the local party meeting there during the Euro elections campaign I had made a favourable impression. While most constituency party meetings can be quite robust, argumentative and occasionally factional, Faversham was something else. I was treated to home-baked scones, home-grown strawberries with lashings of cream and tea in china cups. I have no doubt that, come the socialist revolution when the left rises up and slaughters aristocrats and bankers on our streets, this picturesque corner of Kent will remain untouched – a picture of calm and civility. I politely declined the kind offer to stand for Faversham due to my search for somewhere a tad more winnable than the Kent Tory heartland, but it was nice to feel loved. One thing remained a constant at this time: my union Usdaw and its political officer Ruth Stoney kept faith in me and encouraged me when many others just wanted me out of the way.

Unsurprisingly, the one I really wanted was Southall. But Piara Khabra showed no sign of retiring. He was, after all, only seventy-six years old – or older, if you believe his local enemies who had journeyed to the Punjab to seek out his birth certificate. So, miserable and lonely, I needed to reconcile myself with the fact that I could still make my country a better place through my job in the trade union movement and my role as a Hillingdon borough councillor. Or not.

'Tell me about Gloucester. What's going on down there? Is Tess Kingham going to stand down?'

'There's nothing to tell,' was the reply from the regional officer Roger Hutchinson. His reply never changed, regardless of the number of times I asked him over the late spring period of 2000.

'Anything to report, Roger?'

'Nothing's happening in Gloucester.'

'But someone told me…'

'Nope. Nothing to tell.'

I liked Roger, but I never got the feeling that I was Roger's cup of tea. There is a view among some in the Labour Party that people's representatives in Parliament should have strong local roots in an area. I can understand that. And I can understand why people might see me as a fly-by-night constituency chaser for whom anywhere will do as long as it means they become an MP. I don't know if that was his view of me or not, but I was looking for somewhere to devote my life to – a place I could change, shape and improve immeasurably. In any case, so many of us are now world citizens. My parents were from the Punjab, I was born in London, I supported Liverpool in football and I wanted India to beat England at cricket. Surely, in the modern world, if I could prove to a local party that I was the best candidate and could make the greatest difference to their lives, that's all that should matter?

Sure enough, in the weeks to come, Tess Kingham told the Gloucester Labour Party that she would not stand for a second term as the city's Labour MP. There was now a vacancy to be the candidate in the 2001 general election so, rather than pester

Roger Hutchinson at the regional office (and probably not make much progress), I had a novel idea.

'Hello. Labour South West.'

'Hi, Parmjit here. Could I speak to…'

'I'm afraid Roger's not available.'

'… to Graham Manuel, please.'

Of course. Graham was Roger's quietly spoken boss – hard to read but he knew I'd done a professional job for him in Swindon in 1997. I had to squeeze the phone harder to my ear as Graham was a whisperer.

'Good to hear from you, Parmjit. Gloucester? A bit more diverse down there than people think. There's a guy you should meet. I think he may be from an ethnic minority background too. Chinese, maybe. You should to talk to a guy called … Jonathan Hoad.'

Suddenly, the gloom was about to lift and the greatest adventure of my life was about to begin.

CHAPTER 12

ENGLAND'S GLORY (THE HONOURABLE MEMBER FOR GINSTERS PASTIES)

REGARDLESS OF WHAT MPs tell you, it is not uncommon for them to get lost in their own constituencies. Getting lost on your first visit may be some kind of record, though. My rendezvous point was to be the England's Glory public house. I knew I had arrived when I saw the unique England's Glory matchbox sign, made right here in Middle England, Gloucester.

I parked the car and set about looking for the entrance. It was a strange kind of pub – more like a warehouse.

'Excuse me, mate,' I said to a guy in blue overalls. 'How do I get inside? I could murder a pint.'

He looked at me and without condescension said, 'I think you need to find a pub then. The Linden Tree is good and not far away.'

I was puzzled and pointed up to the sign. 'England's Glory?'

'Oh, the England's Glory! No, my friend, this is the factory where they used to make the matches. You want the pub. It's on London Road.'

Luckily I had built plenty of spare time into my day. I shook off my embarrassment and found my destination. The pub was a short walk from the pedestrianised town centre. It was designed by the Romans for simpletons without a sense of direction (like me) with north, east, south and west laid out in the street names: Northgate Street, Southgate Street, Eastgate Street … and the other one.

It was late afternoon. The sun shone as I wandered down Northgate Street. For a town centre it seemed quiet but oddly pretty, with peculiar church spires at the ends of street corners plus a Kwiksave and a Wilkinson's (and all on a historic Roman street). It was somewhere that looked quite middle class in structure yet with working-class people pulling Sholleys and carrying home groceries in carrier bags on the bus. A bit like home but in a more scenic location – and nothing like as ethnically diverse. I did see black children riding bikes and heard them speaking to each other in a disarmingly soft south-west drawl. There was also a gentleman in a suit carrying an umbrella under one arm and a broadsheet newspaper under the other, a pensioner ferrying a pile of cake tins to her church, and a Muslim woman in a niqab.

It's hard to describe how I felt – but I'll try. I felt a real sense of comfort. Almost immediately I felt at ease and strangely calm. And I don't do calm. I had been warned that Gloucester was a marginal seat; that we only ever won it when we had a Labour government. I knew Peter Mandelson had made a PowerPoint presentation in 1997 that concluded with a picture of Gloucester Cathedral. Victory for Labour and an overall majority of one meant Gloucester Cathedral would have a Labour MP. But, at this moment, I wanted it to be mine. I already knew that I wanted to represent her and her people in Parliament.

'You must be Jonathan Hoad.' I managed to come to that conclusion because there were only three other people in the England's Glory and he was the only one sat alone. Graham Manuel's description had helped give away his identity too. Jonathan's mother is from the north of England and has bright red hair. His father is of Chinese origin but is Jamaican. I've never met his father, but Jonathan has tried to imitate his accent to me. I guess you could say that Jonathan's diverse roots make him very much a world citizen, not just in appearance but in outlook too. In the next couple of hours he would help me map out my life. He'd break off occasionally to speak to people on his mobile, discussing me quite loudly with Kate (his partner) and others while I was still in his presence – 'Yes. I'm talking to one of them right now!' I can't remember the exact conversations but I can recall some of the things about me he came out with: 'He's very tall. Should help catch the Speaker's eye! Be very visible if he's at the rugby – won't have to stand on a box. Seems smooth; ladies will like him. Might be a bit of an urban sophisticate!'

He was a real hoot and, for me, one of those rare things in life: someone I could just let my guard down with and talk to. A special and close friendship began – one that would last a lifetime.

Jonathan asked if I had eaten. Food had become secondary to my quest for a career in politics so, for three reasons, I was happy to take up his offer for dinner. Firstly, it gave me more time to spend with this engaging and educational character. Secondly, it helped me cement my relationship with this key constituency party officer – Jonathan had experience of being the constituency secretary and was now the party treasurer. And thirdly and very crucially, it brought me an introduction to Kate Haigh, his partner.

I feared that giving Jonathan a lift home in my little red Toyota MR2 could put him off my candidature. The car looked like a little red wedge of cheese and was most unbecoming for a would-be MP. But perhaps he saw it as a symbol of my lack of convention – and he didn't strike me as a stickler for convention. When we arrived at his house, Kate and her two young boys, Corin and Jack, greeted me with a combination of warmth and sympathy. Jonathan informed Kate that my car was full of Ginsters wrappers and that I needed to be fed or he feared I'd flake out. I confess that my journey and the route to come would be one Ginsters could have sponsored as I grabbed their sustenance wherever I could, roaming garages for pies in between meeting local party members. But not this evening. I found a home from home at the Hoad household with the acerbic wit of Jonathan Hoad, the tea, sympathy and advice of Kate and the distraction of Jack and Corin. Plus, over dinner that night, Kate drew up a list of people I should talk to.

I went part time at the union and became a regular visitor to the Hoad household. Jack and Corin were perennially amused by my antics. *Does he really sleep in his car and live off Ginsters pasties?* It was only partly true. Phil, an old university friend, now lived in a flat in Clifton, a lively and fun part of Bristol. He had a spare single mattress he let me drag into his lounge to kip on and it only took about half an hour to get to Gloucester from Phil's pad.

A part-time job in London; people to see in Gloucester; a new social life with an old buddy in Bristol … life was changing.

Whatever time I showed up after a day of scurrying around Gloucester, Kate made sure there was a hot meal or slice of cake to keep me from wasting away and, usually over a pint, there was eternal optimism about my candidature from Jonathan in the England's Glory. I never actually asked the Hoads if they would vote for me – not because I took them for granted or doubted them, but because their generosity of spirit was all I needed and I had that in spadefuls.

The timetable had been set for the selection of the new candidate. It would all come to a head over three months in the summer of 2000. I was focused and also, for the first time in a long time, having fun. But always at the back of my mind was a nagging fear: what happens in three months' time if, when this is over, one of the ninety other candidates who have put a CV in actually gets it? What will become of me? How will I cope? This life was all-consuming. Obsessive.

Back in Hayes, after a day's work, my obsession found new ways to manifest itself. On my wall was a map of Gloucester on which I had fastidiously marked in orange day-glo pen the boundaries of every local ward that made up the seat. Post-it notes stuck to each ward told me who I had spoken to and their likelihood to support me. My leatherette-bound notepad contained my findings:

> Longlevens ward. Note: pronounce it Long-levans next time, you fool. NOT Long-leevens! Mr and Mrs Richards are lovely. Joe and Mary too; he's in the union. Kingsholm. Home of the rugby ground. Malcolm is a head teacher. Emma is a teacher too; her partner Richard is constituency secretary. Everton fan. Mark in Linden shares a birthday with me. Steve in Matson used to be a runner.

My wall was becoming a prop from an episode of Robbie Coltrane's *Cracker*. My hunger for information became more intense:

> He is pro-Trident. She was a Greenham Common Woman; passionate about Amnesty International; has a pet dog called Buster. He writes poems about naked women. This person is likely to murder one of the other candidates if he is elected. This lady paints delightful portraits. I never want to be alone in a room with this man, ever.

Little by little, my campaign was starting to take shape.

CHAPTER 13

THE SELECTION BEGINS

THE WAY POLITICAL parties select their parliamentary candidates is interesting. The Labour Party didn't used to trust its members to choose their candidates. A typical party would have, say, 400 paying members. A combination of activists, trade unionists and affiliates to the party, numbering around thirty, would sit on the party's general management committee – the local party's equivalent of the Supreme Soviet Politburo, only with elbow patches on jumpers.

Then John Smith came along as Labour's leader and smashed up this cosy cartel, introducing One Member One Vote (OMOV).

The downside of this initiative was that local parties soon became open to entryism. Families would join en bloc, become silent party members and then jump out of the bushes come selection time. The Labour Party's modern problem is that OMOV has led to local parties in many parts of the country being effectively taken over by groups of voters from one racial or religious group – south Asian politics played out in the UK. In other constituencies, the old vested interests have managed to assert their control and the white, working-class trade unionist is still in charge. Then there is the third, and sadly dwindling, type of seat: constituencies that have a membership broadly representative of those who live in the area, have an open mind about the people they meet (in tune with Labour values), and believe in selection on merit. Refreshingly, Gloucester Labour Party fell in to the latter category.

So, now that Tess Kingham had announced she was retiring, the process had formally begun. The constituency contained a dozen local council wards and each one of them would nominate one man and one woman to the shortlist. The half a dozen affiliated trade union branches did likewise and, from that pool of candidates, the general management committee of about thirty people – a nod to the days of the Supreme Soviet style – would whittle it down to a shortlist of four or six, half men and half women. Then the full party membership would be able to attend a hustings meeting and vote for their preferred candidate.

Because Labour-held seats were in short supply compared to the number of people who wanted them, the Gloucester party found itself deluged with over ninety CVs. Among them were quite a few Euro candidates who had failed to win in the 1999 elections, including at least two former MEPs. There were swathes of councillors from across the country, chief executives of charities, business people … and some random people who couldn't spell. Due to the passing of a former Labour councillor in the Barnwood ward, an opportunity soon arose to test the commitment of the wannabes. The local council by-election gave the party an opportunity to get the would-be MPs out knocking on doors to show their support for Jan Lugg, the council by-election candidate – so I made it my business to be out knocking on doors with Gloucester comrades as often as I could. Those who turned up on members' doorsteps to canvass for their own MP ambitions rather than to put the work in for Jan on the streets of Barnwood got short shrift from activists. It also played to one of my strengths: I like people and I'm good on the doorstep. I could sometimes see party members knocking on adjacent houses and looking over the privet hedge to size me up as I canvassed a voter for 'Jan Lugg – the best thing that has ever happened to Barnwood'. What they saw and heard was this exotic-looking chap from London with peculiar ways but a charming and relaxed manner on the doorstep. Years of training others had helped me. Jonathan would tell people I was like finely oiled silk on the doorstep, which I thought was an unfortunate mixing of metaphors but you got the idea.

Pretty soon the field was breaking down to the serious players. The ninety CVs were out there, but there was only a small group who looked like they could win it. They all had their strengths and weaknesses. Foremost among them was the council leader Kevin Stephens. Kevin had been a candidate before at the 1992 election. He had a fearsome reputation – a council leader of strength and conviction and the first to admit he had as many enemies as friends. I don't think this was actually true: his enemies were just more vocal than his friends. I'd heard a lot about this local man and, at the first 'members meet the candidates' event (a bit like speed dating for parliamentary candidates where you go around and meet the members in a community centre), I went over to say hello to him. I can't remember what I said but I probably asked him if he was having a good night. He told me, with a broad smile, that he knew every single person in the room who would support him and he knew every single one who didn't like him. I sensed Kevin knew his vote share was going to be high, but also that it would have a ceiling. There would not be many second or third preferences for him. People would either be for or against him. Kevin, I understood, came within a vote or two of beating Tess Kingham for the 1997 nomination. He didn't get it and was hurt. He stood down from the council and took some time out. In this selection, his enemies used that against him by reprinting and posting out to the membership a local newspaper article from 1996 about his resignation and the by-election that had resulted. It wasn't a nice thing to see happen, even to a 'rival' in this contest. In my dealings within Kevin he's always shown dignity and a deep loyalty to Gloucester and the Labour Party.

Tess Kingham's assistant Sue Hayman was another serious contender. Common sense dictated that, as the MP's right-hand woman, she would be a big beneficiary of the support for the retiree. She was also very photogenic and well plugged into the party. But her challenge would be a different one: stepping out as someone's number two for the top job in the same patch doesn't always work.

And then there was the hot favourite. Janet Royall had a lifelong association with Gloucester. She was a resident of Blaisdon in the neighbouring parliamentary constituency. She had the backing of the powerful AEEU union and over twenty years' experience working for the Labour Party in the European Parliament, the European Commission, the House of Commons and the leadership of the Labour Party itself. Neil Kinnock's personal endorsement on her full-colour printed glossy leaflet – which contained two pictures of the former party leader himself (my leaflet was run off the colour copier at Chana's chemist in Southall by Dad) – stated:

> Jan is a marvellous mixture of imagination, vitality and common sense. She's a firm realist with great ideals and an endless capacity for hard work and public service. After fifteen years of working together, the only thing that would make her absence bearable is the knowledge that she'd be a Labour MP. And that she'd be a *great* one, especially when she's got the extra vital ingredient of local understanding and commitment.

Now, knowing Jan myself, I can vouch for all of that too – but, thankfully, I only read that leaflet today for the first time. For fourteen years it's sat in a box with other bits and bobs, including leaflets by the other candidates who applied for Gloucester. If I had read it then I probably wouldn't have had the bottle to stand against her.

Among the others who were particularly visible in the selection process were: Ian White, former MEP for Bristol; Anne Snelgrove, who had been on the same Euro list as me in the south-east and went on to become MP for Swindon South in 2005; Peter Herbert, a prominent black lawyer; and Keir Dhillon, a local trade union official. Plus many, many others who deserve a mention but, alas, *My Political Race* is not *War and Peace*.

Kevin Stephens, Sue Hayman and Janet Royall started to rattle up nominations among some of the local wards and union branches. But so did a fourth candidate. He was twenty-eight years old, a councillor from the London borough of Hillingdon, a former Euro candidate and the assistant national organiser for a telecoms trade union called Connect. He was powered by a combination of adrenalin, watermelon Bacardi Breezers and late nights at Po Na Na nightclub in Bristol – plus, I guess, a slightly dangerous mix of ability and lack of self-confidence that he could ever pull off a heist like this. That was me. In fact, as Sue Hayman and Jan Royall ratcheted up the nominations on the women's side, something extraordinary was happening on the men's side. For Kevin, the support among his councillors was loyal and solid. He represented Matson ward and he lived in Linden – both of which he won. Keir Dhillon won in Quedgeley and a chap called Peter Drousiotous won the majority support of the members of the Podsmead ward.

I was delighted to win in the Abbeymead ward as this meant I would be through to the Politburo stage where they would draw up the shortlist. Then I won Barnwood ward and Eastgate too. I was thrilled. I took Kate and Jonathan's ward Kingsholm, as expected. And Longlevens. Then Westgate. And Hucclecote too. One or two wards for lack of a quorum didn't nominate anybody but, in a constituency of thirteen wards where I had no roots or connections, I'd taken eight wards plus three trade union nominations. I actually had more nominations than the other men put together.

But my nemesis was soon to strike again. I was soon to be taken down some pegs and made to feel humiliated – the outsider in somebody else's game. It would leave me to decide whether to be a good boy and trudge off home alone while the others played, or to dig my heels in.

CHAPTER 14

MY DILEMMA

THE CALL CAME from someone I knew well, someone I trusted and someone who was well plugged into the party machine. A senior officer of the national Labour Party at Millbank Tower wanted a message conveyed to me. In blunt terms it was this: 'You've had your fun, but now you need to get out of the way so someone who is serious about winning the selection can get it. You are seen as a distraction and there's a danger that Kevin Stephens will be selected if you don't move aside.'

As I had expected, the party was closely monitoring selections in its seats, and the number of nominations I had picked up had obviously caused a spike in their interest. But it didn't make sense. Firstly because Kevin wasn't what they thought he was and, in any case, the voting system was an exhaustive ballot where you got to vote first, second, third preference etc., so why was my candidature likely to help one candidate more than any another? The fact that it was even suggested I shouldn't be fighting the selection unsettled me.

Something else that was passed on to me made my heart sink even further: *What's he doing down there anyway? Why doesn't he wait for somewhere more suitable like Ealing Southall or somewhere in Birmingham?*

I had a few problems with this.

Firstly, if they really wanted me in one of those 'ethnic seats' they had a funny way of showing it. After only just surviving Stoke Rochford Hall, I wasn't optimistic about a helping hand with jam tomorrow.

Secondly, perhaps they just thought I wasn't up to it. What if they were right?

Thirdly, perhaps it wasn't personal. Was I just in the way of a preferred candidate and they thought it was easy to push me around because I was young?

Fourthly, and most worryingly, perhaps in the year 2000 they just weren't ready for ethnic minority candidates in white seats. Maybe they thought it was too much of a risk in Gloucester. Would I be contributing to my party losing its key seat by fighting on?

Was it a combination of all these things?

I don't believe that any of the candidates in the selection contest were involved in what was happening to me. But I was now sinking to rock-bottom when I should have been on a high. Don't believe anyone who tells you it's better to have loved and lost than never to have loved at all. I felt Gloucester slipping away from me. The fact that my confidence was shaken by this made me doubt myself even more. I went back home to Hayes and my parents.

For a day I ignored calls and messages from my new friends in Gloucester who were brimming with ideas of people I should meet or places I should see. I had a couple of days back at work for the union and was trying to readjust. If I was destined to lose anyway, wouldn't it be better to leave the contest now? Maybe my detractors were right to think I was all wrong for the constituency. I remember going back to my bedroom and feeling unloved by the party I loved.

I looked at the map of Gloucester with the day-glo markings of the wards; the scraps of paper and the Post-it notes all over the wall; the lists of people I'd met. Wasn't it really up to them? Shouldn't the members decide who the best person to be their candidate is? If I walked away, could I trust the Labour Party to help me elsewhere? I didn't sense I was their kind of person. I couldn't trust them. If I stayed in the contest would they turn their backs on me for ever? They could. But they couldn't if I won. If I won, they'd be queuing up to say how great I was.

So stuff them. I got back into my little red car and back into the race.

· · ·

My wobble was over and I was more determined than ever. The general management committee reduced the candidates to a shortlist and I was hoping it would be a list of four. I had done enough to be one of the top two men and I wanted a clear choice. Four makes the decision simpler than six. But they chose six. Some strong candidates who just hadn't picked up enough nominations fell by the wayside, including Libby Lisgo and Peter Herbert.

It was to be Jan Royall, Sue Hayman and Sue Mallory on the female side; the men were Kevin Stephens, Keir Dhillon and myself. While the voting took place I mingled with the other candidates. I was pleased not to have got into disagreements with any of them thus far in the campaign and was determined to keep it that way. There were a couple of reasons for this. Firstly, because I'd obviously been brought up to be a nice man, and, secondly, because the least unpopular person often comes through to win these contests due to the transferable voting system.

I found myself in the bar of the civil service club having a pint with Kevin. I commiserated with him over the hostility he'd faced from some of those in the party – something that can go hand in hand with being the local boy. It was a good chat. We were both in a reflective mood after some chastening moments in this long selection process. I confided my fears that I wouldn't make the shortlist and he reassured me that I would. I had so many nominations that it would be 'against the tenets of natural justice' if I wasn't chosen. The time I'd spent in Southall politics had left me sniffing for stitch-ups to block out good candidates, but he was right: this was open and fair-minded Gloucester. He and I had comfortably crossed the line to get on the shortlist, and so had Sue and Jan.

Later that night I received a text message from one of the local party's officers. We got on well, although he had kept a professional neutrality through the contest. He texted just five words but it told me things were starting to tip my way: 'It's got to be you.'

There was now just over a week to go until the hustings. I had to reinvigorate things to pull this off. I did not want to leave this place. Not now, not ever.

CHAPTER 15

MOMENTUM

THE ENGLAND'S GLORY public house was where it had begun for me a few months earlier. It's where I'd met Jonathan Hoad and where the ball had started rolling for me. Labour may have won the Gloucester parliamentary seat back from the Tories in 1997 for the first time since 1970, but all was not well. I sensed local party members yearned for the spirit of the old days. They needed a new sense of purpose as a united party, without factions and with a common cause to unite behind. They talked about the days when the England's Glory was a hotbed of Labour activism. Activists, party members and councillors would congregate there, socialise and plot the downfall of our common enemy – the Tories. Since 1997, the local MP had fallen out of love with Parliament, the local campaigning base was weaker than it should have been and cliques were emerging in the local party.

My campaign was inclusive and fresh – being an outsider had its advantages as well as its downsides. I also had momentum. When I visited members they greeted me warmly and would often say they had heard good things about me. They seemed as eager to hear from me as I was to hear from them. So I continued with more confidence than ever, but never really imagining victory or expecting to pull it off. It was more like playing a game; it was easier on my mind that way or else I would've had to think about defeat and what that would mean for me. I set my mind on one more push to see me through to the big day, Friday 28 July 2000 – the day of the selection at Shire Hall. And what better place to make that push than the England's Glory pub, where I could become a link for Gloucester activists between an insurgent future and a happier past? It would also be my last real opportunity to say thank you and, in all likelihood, goodbye.

So we set a date just a few nights before the selection for a get-together. Kate Haigh and others worked feverishly to contact people who were warm towards me – as well as those yet to meet me – and invited them all to the England's Glory.

On the night, a nice gathering of half a dozen people showed up. That then became two dozen. The pub was soon bristling with Labour people. By chance, Sue Hayman and her husband popped in for dinner but decided not to stay. I urged her to hang about and have a drink but, understandably, she said she felt it was my night to do whatever I was doing. And it was. People who hadn't seen each other for years were now back together in the England's Glory. There was a buzz about it; it was like old times. By the end of the night I'd say between thirty and forty Labour members had come in to talk to me about their policy concerns or just to say hello and wish me luck. It gave me even greater impetus to work harder in the coming days and meet more members.

In my mind a vision was coming together for this historic Roman city. The peaceful but decaying Gloucester docks were at the forefront of it. This city had fallen under the shadow of neighbouring Cheltenham in recent years but whoever could unlock the potential of the docks could transform this place economically, creating jobs, retail and leisure facilities. It was a beautiful place, even if many locals didn't see it that way. With a bit more working-class pride, the right investment in public services – the hospital, the college, the schools, the police station – and a focus on skills and higher education, Gloucester's potential had no limits. A young city with promise for the twenty-first century.

I kept my focus on conversations with local party members. Keith and Elaine Waldon took me in for coffee and biscuits and briefed me on the history of Gloucester's divided education system. They had long campaigned for the local comprehensives in a constituency that contained four grammar schools. They would become lifelong friends, regular babysitters for my then unborn children and very close friends with my partner, whom I was still yet to meet. I visited Kay and Roger Mills, who had already committed their support to Jan Royall, but I wanted to meet everyone, whoever they supported, because I could still learn something from them. After many failed attempts to get an appointment with them, Kay Mills relented and said I could pop round if I was in the neighbourhood before she went out shopping. As usual, I parked my little red MR2 out of sight before going to the Mills abode. It so wasn't the right car for a would-be candidate. Kay and Roger, I discovered, are the kind of people who have kept constituency parties up and down the land alive since the Labour Party was formed. Kay had been a Greenham Common Woman in the 1980s. Roger had built a mock cruise missile that had toured the country warning of the perils of the nuclear holocaust. They'd both dropped out of activism in the party in recent years but just needed to be asked to come back. It was the most extraordinary afternoon.

The Kays and Rogers of the Labour Party don't just give time to the cause, they devote their lives to it. Their three grown-up sons had spent their childhood involved in their campaigns. I don't suppose Dan, Dom or Johnny quite knew why they were dressed in white, lying still on a pavement in silence with hundreds of other people while someone drew around them with chalk. Not at the time, anyway. But how else are you to get across to the British people what was likely to happen in the event of the four-minute warning going off? The Millses may not have won the battle over unilateral nuclear disarmament but their spirits remained undimmed. After a generation of raising a few quid from quiz nights and jumble sales to fight the no-hope ward of Hucclecote in deepest Middle England, you might have thought they'd become jaded. Not so. The Labour Party runs through people like Kay and Roger like the lettering in a stick of rock. They were the warmest and most incredible people you'll ever meet and were to become the bedrock of my new life in Gloucester one day.

After a couple of hours of tea and yet more cakes, I thought I should make my apologies so Kay could actually do her shopping. But, before I did, she pulled out a copy of my campaign leaflet. I thought Chana's chemist in Southall had done a reasonable job on it: 'Parmjit Dhanda – youth, energy and experience for Gloucester.'

'I think we're coming round to you. Aren't we, Rog?'

Roger nodded. 'It's just your time, Parmjit.'

I hadn't expected that. They had known, admired and quite rightly respected Jan Royall for very many years – indeed, as I do now – and, coming from the top of the party, her support was deserved through sheer quality and experience.

Perhaps now I needed to start believing in myself.

CHAPTER 16

28 JULY 2000 –
SHIRE HALL OR BUST

CHIPS AND CHEESE at the Twigworth Inn on Tewkesbury Road. It was a regular routine for me and actually healthier than a lot of the crap I'd eaten on the road over the past three months. The clock was ticking. I gave my mentor Ruth from Usdaw another call.

'I hope they don't make me go first. Last would be best.'

'No, don't worry about that. First is good, you can set the standard. Last out of six would be good too. You don't want to be, say, fourth.'

'I bet I'll get fourth.'

'Parmjit, you've done really well regardless of what happens. Just try to relax and enjoy it.'

It was sound advice but my stomach was churning. My preparation had been good, though. I was very happy with my speech and had practised it many times. I'd rehearsed every possible question the audience could pose and felt I had an answer for everything. I had even visited the council chamber of Shire Hall, where the hustings would take place, to get a feel for it.

It was a grand old room with rows of concentric semi-circular seats, each row raised higher than the previous in a theatre style. There were banks of chairs and tables in the wings of the council chamber too, usually used by press and spectators at council meetings. In the centre was a two-tiered dais facing the rows of seats. The lower tier was for clerks, the chairperson and timekeepers. The higher tier directly behind it was for the speaker addressing those assembled. The mood was mellow when I visited – just a few senior citizens peeling oranges and paying little attention to whoever it was speaking about watercourses or speed humps in the Cotswolds. Welcome to Gloucestershire County Council! I swear there were a couple of octogenarians having a kip on the back row too.

I knew tonight it would be very different, but I liked the feel of the place – its light, its acoustics, the dark wood. If I wanted to be a Member of Parliament I needed to be able to perform on stages like this.

It was 5.45 p.m. and I needed to get to Shire Hall for 6 p.m. As I walked down Tewkesbury Road I realised I hadn't appreciated quite how far away it was. The sight of a lanky Asian man in a pin-striped Reiss suit and red tie running down the road raised a few eyebrows in the Kingsholm area. I'd cut it very close.

By the time I got to Northgate Street I was out of breath and having a mild panic attack. I'd convinced myself I was miles from my destination and that I was about to be excluded from the selection meeting.

Years later, when I was doing some canvassing in the Tuffley area, a man came to the door and we had the following conversation:

'Hi, I'm Parmjit – the local Labour MP. I was wondering…'

'Ah, Parmjit Dhanda! At last we meet again!' (Now, you meet a lot of people as a local MP so I didn't recognise him – but he certainly knew me.) 'Parmjit. When you were lost and in a panic on the selection night on Northgate Street I'm the guy you asked for directions.'

Stone me, it was. He went on to say he could have changed a little bit of history by sending me the wrong way that night. I'm pleased to say that he was glad he hadn't. And so was I.

That night, he had calmed me down and told me I was only 200 yards from Shire Hall. I felt a lot better, although I did come across as a complete buffoon for having such a poor sense of direction and having to ask where I was in a place I wanted to represent!

As I went up the steps of the austere and imposing Shire Hall I could see people pouring in for the selection meeting. My earlier scare over my lack of a sense of direction had subsided and I was now in a more relaxed mood. At least the evening would be a partial success – I was guaranteed a place in the top six. Anything seemed like a bonus compared to 'We had to lock him out as he got lost.'

Steve Richards, the Labour Party's organiser for the area and a really decent man, met me at the top of the stairs and ushered me towards a side room.

'What kept you?'

'Oh, you know. Just needed a walk. Wanted to clear my head.'

It felt like my heartbeat had settled from 200 beats per minute on Northgate Street to a less tense 100.

The side room was actually a very big yet cosy area with sofas against the walls and a table at the end where they would be counting the votes in a few hours' time. It would also be our prison for the next four hours. Each candidate would escape its confines for twenty-five minutes to address the party members for ten minutes and then take questions for a quarter of an hour. We drew lots to decide on the running order. I remembered what Ruth had told me: don't worry if you're near the start or the end; it's, say, number four you don't want. I took my rolled-up piece of paper from Steve Richards and couldn't believe my luck. I got number four.

So I settled down in a quiet corner with the Sony Discman I'd borrowed from my brother. Headphones on, I retreated into my own world with two tracks that I played over and over again. I won't pretend to have the coolest taste in music, but that night wasn't about cool. For me to win I had to blow them away. Passion and noise were what I needed and Catatonia's 'Road Rage' did the trick. The other track that revved me up that night, in the days before it became a populist track used at party conferences, was 'Place Your Hands' by Reef. I must have come across as really antisocial to the other five candidates as they chatted over tea and biscuits, but I just wanted to collect my thoughts and get into a 'zone'.

From recollection, Keir Dhillon was the first one to leave us for the council chamber to do his spiel and take his questions. From our room you could hear the applause after the speech and again after the questions. Not raucous, but polite and warm. He was puffing when he came back, with sweat on his brow, but he seemed happy. Then it was one of the big guns – Kevin Stephens. I wasn't going to let my mind play tricks on me by gauging the level of applause each candidate got. This was not the clap-o-meter from *Opportunity Knocks*. I just concentrated on Catatonia. When Kevin came back in I took off the headphones and stretched my legs.

'They're a good audience,' he beamed. 'They don't want anyone to fail. No nasty questions, you'll all get a good crack at it.' That was reassuring. The only questions I feared were ones about my back-ground, which could sow seeds of doubt about my suitability. No matter how much they might like me, maybe some would shy away from voting for me at the last moment if they thought a brown face in a white seat could spell defeat for the party at the general election.

Sue Hayman was next up. She looked nervous, but who could blame her? If you weren't nervous on a night like this there must be something wrong with you. I went back to listening to 'Road Rage'. It sounds corny, I know, but the music really seemed to help me. It was, and is, a tub-thumping tune that got my adrenalin going. I took a break from it to gather my thoughts one last time. I had written my speech out on little cards, but the cards were now just prompts – a comfort blanket in case nerves got the better of me. I had five minutes to go so I put on the headphones and listened to Reef one last time. Loud.

By the time the track finished I felt ready. I felt like a caged ani-mal, eager to get in there and tear it up. I wasn't going to mess this up. I had convinced myself by now that I had nothing to lose and I had to go for it. It's what Dad had told me to do when I'd rung him earlier that day. Mum had been more pensive, worried about how I'd cope with defeat.

Sue returned. I waited. Steve Richards came to collect me. It was my turn. By now, we were well into the evening and it was dark outside. Steve led me to the brightly lit council chamber. There was silence as I walked in. I caught a few gazes, some smiles. I could feel all eyes trained on me. A pensioner I had met in Westgate at his home – an old union official – gave me a thumbs-up as I was about to walk past him. I didn't stop but I slowed down enough to put my hand on his shoulder as I went by and gave it a gentle squeeze. It was probably against the rules to have 'contact' with the selectorate, but it was instinctive. My suit was buttoned up. My shirt was blue and my tie clean, new and red.

I stood at the dais as the regional officer Roger Hutchinson went through the motions of telling me how long I would be allowed to speak for before a light came on to stop me and how long I had for questions. It was ironic that the man who kept telling me 'There's nothing happening in Gloucester' was now taking charge of the process that would decide my fate. Roger was sat directly in front of me on a lower tier and was to chair the proceedings. Alongside him was the young constituency secretary Richard Price who had become a friend in recent weeks. He had remained professionally neutral throughout, but I knew he wanted to see me do well. Richard had confided in Kate and Jonathan that, although he admired me, this was the big test. He had no idea if I could cut it when it came to the hustings. In Gloucester, every vote had to be earned. But, on the plus side, at least the membership would be open-minded enough to give you the chance to earn it. That's all I could ask for. Roger gave me the signal to go.

Looking back, I wish I'd kept a copy of the speech I gave, or the precise results of the ballot that ensued. Maybe I'll find them both when I least expect it. After all, like most good Indian parents, mine preserve our bedrooms at home so there's minimal change whenever we return to stay for a night. Fifteen years later, the wallpaper hasn't changed in my former bedroom because that would mean shifting my map of Gloucester from the wall. It's still there, day-glo markings and all. Once a decade, though, my parents are entitled to warn us that they're going to clear out some stuff, so my speech from that night and the ballot results may never actually resurface. Oddly enough, every photo of me as a child with long hair or a top knot wrapped in a pink handkerchief is impossible to lose and shows up every time they have visitors. Anyway, I digress. Back to the most important night of my life...

Me in 1976

I looked around the chamber and thanked them all. I thanked them for the warmth of the reception they gave me when I arrived in the city just a few weeks ago and I thanked them for the volume of nominations the branches had given me. The chamber was packed to the rafters. I think there must have been around a couple of hundred people there. I didn't have time to worry about it, but I felt a pang of concern because I didn't recognise most of the people there. I looked around the chamber as I spoke and saw Kay Mills' warm and friendly face. She smiled at me.

I also said that, although it had been an amazing few weeks, I wanted it to be the beginning of a new journey. I wanted to live there, to represent them and to one day have children who would grow up there in a school system that wasn't just about the grammars but would give comprehensive school kids a fair chance too. The nodding heads told me I was striking a chord. I talked about the local Tories who had chosen their council group leader as their candidate. He was even younger than I was and would have a young team of enthusiastic door-knockers going to every door in the constituency. But he didn't have my energy or my campaigning experience and I was ready to put my key-seat skills to use at once for Gloucester Labour.

And I talked of hope. Of potential. I told them that whoever could unlock the potential of the docks would change Gloucester forever. I was impressed by the Labour councillors and the work they were doing there. I was a councillor myself in London and I felt we could all work together as a strong and united party to tap into Gloucester's potential.

Finally, I talked about me and what made me tick. I worked for a trade union and my trade union values had been handed down from my father, who'd come here from India to escape poverty and drive trucks, and my mother, who had spent a lifetime as a NUPE shop steward at the hospital she cleaned. I couldn't change who or what I was, but whatever I had I would dedicate to serving them:

> There'll be no distance between us – local MP and con-stituency party. I want you to be my strength here in the constituency and I want you to be my conscience when I vote in Westminster. And together, let's keep Gloucester Labour. For good.

As I uttered those last two words the light flashed on Roger Hutch-inson's desk and rapturous applause began. I knew I had pitched it spot-on in terms of timing and spot-on in terms of content and delivery. I looked around and saw many people smiling as they looked at me directly or at each other. Some people were even a little emotional (or perhaps relieved) that I had achieved something here. Then Roger Hutchinson did me a massive inadvertent favour. He said, over the microphone: 'Now we know how it should be done.' I don't think he was talking about my speech – he wouldn't have said that even if he meant it – but I suspect they'd had some problems with his timing light or the microphone. Either way, it didn't do me any harm. 'OK,' he said. 'Time for the questions.'

I leant forward and told him I thought it was warm in the room and asked if I could take off my jacket. He said OK. It was some-thing I'd done at every hustings I had attended when fighting the Euro selections and it had never done me any harm.

First up was Keith Waldon. He asked me what my first Private Member's Bill would be. Frankly, I had no idea, but I bought myself time by saying it wouldn't be a bill to ban hunting with hounds because hopefully the Labour government would already have agreed to do that by then! That went down well with the audience, but then I came up with something. I said I felt the councillors locally were doing a good job but had been frustrated time and again in big regeneration projects. I'd look to see if there were more powers government could give them to make it easier.

One down. So far, so good.

The next one was about the role of Europe in our lives. As a former Euro candidate I got through that. Less focus on straight bananas and more on the positive role Europe has played in our lives. My generation grew up with exchange trips to Europe and wanted the chance to work around the world, sampling different cultures. The EU had kept the peace and made that possible, and we should make the case for it.

Two down. No problems.

Then there was one from a group of party members who were in the Fire Brigades Union. What did I think about their right to strike as an emergency service? What a tricky one. I was thoughtful and didn't rush my reply. This is the type of question that can skewer you if you don't think it through or if you're not genuine in your reply. And it did skewer some of the other candidates. I said that obviously I worked for a trade union myself but I felt that strikes were a sign of failure – failure on the part of the employer and failure on the part of the employee representatives. However, in a world with unscrupulous employers, it would be wrong to outlaw strikes entirely. To withdraw your labour is a last resort, but also a fundamental human right in a civilised society.

The final question was from Mr Hakim and it was the question I had feared – a question that could have been ruled out of order. Mr Hakim is a lovely man and has been good to me so I think he genuinely thought he was being helpful. 'Mr Parmjit, what makes you think you can win here? There are very few people from minorities in Gloucester, and they are mostly Muslim like me. What makes you believe as a Sikh from outside the area that you can win?' I could only see three faces that weren't white in the chamber, so he did have a point.

I'm glad Roger didn't rule the question out – it would have left it hanging in the air. This was the last question and I couldn't afford to mess up the answer and go out on a low when everything to this point had gone so well.

So I just let my answer flow as it came into my head, and it came out like this:

> We're the Labour Party. We don't believe in doing the easy thing but doing the right thing. I don't want favours from any of you. If you think I'm the best, then choose me. If I'm not, then choose someone else. In any case, for years we've talked about better representation of society in Parliament. But it always seems to be about somewhere else. Well, if not here, then where? And if not now, then when?

That was it. In the momentary silence I looked at the audience. Some heads nodded.

Roger Hutchinson broke the silence: 'Parmjit Singh Dhanda, thank you.'

I left the chamber and let myself enjoy the applause. But I took nothing for granted. On the way out I stopped to shake the outstretched hand of the elderly trade union official from Westgate – probably breaking the rules again in doing so.

CHAPTER 17

I WON'T BE
HOME TONIGHT

SUE MALLORY AND Janet Royall were still to come. I was now relaxed – I had done all I could – but in the back of my mind was something the young black MP for Bethnal Green & Bow had written in an article I'd read somewhere. Oona King said she had won other hustings meetings prior to her triumph in east London, but she hadn't gone on to win the ballot. In other words, she may have put in the best performance, but she didn't get the votes.

Soon, Sue and Jan had taken their turns and the proceedings in the chamber had concluded – at least until the announcement of the winner. Our private room had become the domain of party officers, appointed counting agents, party staff, candidates and their partners (those who were lucky enough to have them). There were about twenty people in the room now; the rest were locked out while the counting began, starting with the postal votes. One after another, the party members who had been in the council chamber for the speeches came over to tell me they thought I'd performed really well. Keir Dhillon came over to say he knew he'd done well but that he'd heard mine was the best speech. Richard Price had lost his veneer of neutrality: 'You nailed it, mate. Well done. Bloody injustice if you're not the winner.'

As the postal votes were counted I soon realised I'd cocked up. Badly. I was so confident that the good folk of Gloucester would turn up on the night and listen intently that I had forgotten the importance of organisation. Inexcusable and naive for a former organiser. Of the four candidates most fancied to have a chance of victory, I was last, with just four or five postal voters voting for me as their first preference. I was over twenty votes behind Jan Royall and left with a mountain to climb. I was pretty resigned to my fate and walked away from the table, leaving my two counting agents Frank Kelly and Mike Williams to look out for my interests. The postal votes were added to the first preferences of the people who had actually attended the hustings. As they totted them up, Frank came over, gave me encouragement and told me I was doing well. The last thing I needed was somebody trying to cheer me up. Oona King, I thought. Maybe my day will never come.

The ballot papers had my full name on them – Parmjit Singh Dhanda. Mum always told me to be proud of my full Sikh name. Well, it looked like Parmjit Singh Dhanda was about to go down in flames.

Steve Richards called the candidates over to the table to announce the result of the first preferences and to tell us who had been knocked out. Sue Mallory and Keir Dhillon had finished in the bottom two and their combined total didn't add up to the fourth-placed candidate's total so they were both knocked out. With the postal votes added to the votes from the council chamber, Kevin Stephens was fourth with a healthy tally of around forty votes. He was just behind Sue Hayman by one or two votes. In second place was Jan Royall with about forty-five votes. I was in first place with around forty-nine. I had clawed back the postal votes deficit and taken the lead due to the people who had witnessed our contributions that night.

I was shocked. But it was close and I didn't dare believe I could win it, despite the excitement of some of the people around me. Then the dozen or so votes Mallory and Dhillon had accrued together were redistributed. Kevin wasn't a beneficiary of second preferences; the bulk went to me. Kevin Stephens was eliminated and I had opened up a bigger lead, with Sue Hayman and Jan picking up a couple of votes apiece. Each time Steve Richards announced the results he double-barrelled my surname: 'Mr Singh Dhanda – fifty-eight.'

Richard Price and Frank were on my shoulders now, encouraging me, but I was too tense to smile or even pay close attention. 'It's not going to happen, Rich. Kevin and Sue's votes won't distribute to me.'

Kevin was upset. It got more tense in the room but his lovely wife Anne was there to calm him down. When you've spent your life working your socks off for your local party I guess it's natural to feel let down when your local party doesn't choose you. I felt for him. But I felt for myself too. The longer I was in the race, the more Shakespearian this tragedy was destined to be. Kevin's votes were the next ones to be redistributed. Quite a lot of his voters were so loyal to him that they didn't use their second preferences and where the others would go was anybody's guess. My prediction was that they would stay local, so not for me. But I was wrong. With just Sue Hayman, Jan Royall and me left in the race, they split in my favour again. That meant something. The local councillors, who were largely loyal to Kevin, were showing me some support. I had around eighty votes now. Round by round, my lead was growing over Jan, who was in the sixties. Sue was eliminated.

I could hardly breathe. People were now crowding around me. People were telling me I was going to win it. *No. The MP is a woman. Sue's support will go en bloc to Jan. They want a woman.* I just didn't want to die of a broken heart that night. After the eighteen months I'd just had, something was bound to go wrong.

Steve Richards was commentating aloud on every remaining ballot paper as people crowded around the table. More people seemed to have snuck in from somewhere. Steve's soft Welsh voice could be heard in the hush from everyone around the table as he redistributed the votes: 'Royall, Singh Dhanda, Singh Dhanda, Royall, Singh Dhanda, Singh Dhanda…'

At one point he looked straight up at me as if to say 'You're over the threshold'. At that moment I knew. And then the votes kept flowing. In the end I think I was on 118 and Jan was in the high eighties or nineties. Steve declared the figures to the room and said: 'The winning candidate is Parmjit Singh Dhanda.'

I'd done it. There were many hands to shake and people to hug but my first priority was to commiserate with each of the other candidates. Jan would go on to become Baroness Royall of Blaisdon and a member of the Cabinet as leader of the House of Lords. Defeat to me in a marginal seat may have been the best thing that could have happened for her. Kevin became one of my stalwarts and continued as leader of Gloucester City Council for a few more years; Keir was a regular on the doorsteps with me too; and Sue Hayman has recently been selected in the Labour seat of Workington. Alas, I lost touch with Sue Mallory.

They were all good, able people and I wish them the best of luck in all of their endeavours. I hope they don't mind me writing about them, but I can't write about my own story without mentioning the important connection they have to it.

Most of the party members, refreshed from a trip to the neighbouring public houses, were back in the chamber awaiting the result, so I was led to the podium to be announced as the successful candidate. I made a short speech thanking them, promising not to let them down and informing them that I'd be at the party office at 10 a.m. in the morning to start work – and would welcome their presence. I think I should have left out the last bit … or at least made it 11 a.m.

Stunned, on the steps of Shire Hall with Ruth of Usdaw

After the selection, celebration at the Hoads'

It was hugs-and-kisses time. I felt a wave of emotion as members I knew, had briefly met or had never seen before came to congratulate me. Among the congratulations came one from a member whom I won't name:

'Well done. You were the best.'

'I'm really grateful for your support.'

'Oh, I didn't vote for you. I couldn't because I think you'll lose the seat. Too many racists around here.'

And then, out of the corner of my eye, I saw Ruth Stoney. She'd travelled down from the Usdaw offices and came running towards me looking elated. I was so pleased to be able to hug the person who had taken such a gamble on me and I'll be eternally grateful to her and to Usdaw.

But there was no time to hang around. Steve Richards led me away to speak to the local newspaper on the phone. Thankfully Kate Haigh was there to spread her maternal wings around me and she started arranging for people who wanted to stay up late and celebrate to make their way to her home and indulge in the car boot full of booze that Ruth had picked up already. As I made my way behind Steve down the staircase in Shire Hall I just had to stop for a moment. I'm a good Indian boy and good Indian boys need to ring their parents.

So, there and then on the stairwell, as I waved and smiled at people walking past, I knew I needed to let Mum and Dad know. It was late; they would be in bed. I was a bit worried – they are the type of parents who cry easily. When we were kids, if Budgie, Parminder or I came home from school with a good report they would well up with tears of pride and carry it around in their pockets to show our uncles and aunts. Pass a driving test – tears; get into a university – tears; not get thrown out of university – a celebration at the gurdwara and tears. I didn't mind: I lived to make them proud. But, as an event, this was UK history, let alone big news in the Asian community.

Dad answered: '*Ha poth. Kiddha*? How are you?' He was trying to sound calm and reassuring but I could feel he was on tenterhooks. He was hoping for good news but the timbre of his voice was one to comfort me from bad news. A voice can give away so much more than words.

'I'm OK, Dad.' There was still something of a din going on around me so I had to squeeze the phone closer to my ear. 'Dad, I want you to stay calm and not get too excited.' Some hope! 'Look, I'm not coming home tonight. I got it...'

I can still hear his muffled gasp of emotion today when I think about the call. He went quieter still and I could just about hear him choking back tears and telling Mum. 'He done it! *Sudar munda bungaya*!' – or, translated: 'Our boy's done it!' He didn't yell; it was a kind of an elation-mixed-with-shock sound – but it set my mother off too. Hers was more of a high-pitched shriek.

As Dad was still trying to choke back the tears, I felt the need to make sure they didn't get too emotional:

'I haven't won anything yet. Got to work hard. But we've got an 8,000 majority so I should become an MP. Can you let Budgie and Parminder know?'

'Can I tell them?'

'Yes. You can tell them. Pretty much everyone will know soon.'

Steve Richards was trying to get me to take another call so I promised to ring back when things calmed down a bit and to visit the gurdwara at the weekend, as Mum was insisting. I also agreed to come home the following day so friends, neighbours and family could drink champagne or whisky with me.

There were many calls and texts that night – from close friends, from Labour people and from people I hardly knew – but before I put down the phone to Dad he said: 'We're really proud of you, son.'

At the age of twenty-eight, I could have died a happy man that night.

CHAPTER 18

THE OFFENDING ARTICLE

I T HAD BEEN just a few weeks since the selection. I was adjusting to my new life. My priorities were simple: buy a flat as quickly as possible in the constituency; heal any rifts from the selection process; and cut down on work commitments in London so I could devote myself to the doorsteps of Gloucester. My new local party was wonderfully supportive, my employers were as accommodating as you could hope for and all seemed to be settling down nicely.

When Kate Haigh phoned me at work on the afternoon of Friday 8 August 2000, I sensed it was going to be bad news – she wasn't her usual chirpy self. I wasn't wrong. She had seen an article in the *Gloucester Citizen* newspaper that she needed to tell me about.

It was to become an article that would leave a mark on me for life. Locally and nationally, in newspapers and even on TV programmes, it would be oft-quoted. I was once hosted by political writers in Washington as they debated it. The effect it had on me as a young man without a political hide to protect me was deep. But, looking back, you could argue it may have done me more good than harm. You'll have to be the judge of that.

The issues it raised could not be left unchallenged. My maiden speech in Parliament would one day be given meaning by the many falsehoods it painted about me, my local party and my constituents. On the plus side, the article galvanised the Gloucester Labour Party and made it more determined to win than ever. But I could have done without it – it was not the kind of coverage I ever envisaged or wanted. Its author, Hugh Worsnip, articulated a widely held private view – shared by too many people in party political establishments – that ethnic minority candidates should not represent white areas. With the rise of UKIP in more recent years, and the ensuing desire to find a political response, I hear Worsnip's sentiments again from people who should know better – people of influence who have shunned racial diversity because of perceived political risk.

I still find it hard when I read the article in full to explain how I felt at the time. All I can suggest is that you put yourself in my shoes and imagine you're reading somebody talking about you like this to the people you're trying to convince to make you their local

MP. You can judge for yourself whether it was racist, a fuss about nothing or something else entirely.

A RIGHT ROYALL MISTAKE

The more I learn about the selection of the Labour Party's candidate to fight the next general election in Gloucester, the more convinced I become that they can kiss goodbye to the seat.

They might as well hand it over to the Conservative candidate Paul James now.

In phone calls and emails, Labour stalwarts are telling me choosing Mr Parmjit Singh Dhanda, a Sikh from London, was actually a mistake caused by the complicated voting system used at the members' general meeting a fortnight ago.

Apparently, there was stunned silence at the meeting when Mr Dhanda won, because many thought that the successful candidate was going to be Janet Royall. Under the fifth ballot, under the complicated transferable vote system used by super-democratic New Labour, there were about ten votes in it.

Things were so much easier when candidates were picked by a handful of party elders in a smoke-filled room rather than the whole party membership of between 400 and 500 people.

I gather that the very capable trade union organiser Mr Dhanda produced, at the crucial meeting, a tub-thumping political harangue in the very best traditions of socialism.

But will enough typical working-class voters in Gloucester put their crosses down next general election day for Mr Dhanda? I very much doubt it.

The Labour Party in Gloucester has made the same mistake as the Tories in Cheltenham when they chose black barrister John Taylor as their candidate and handed the seat to the Liberal Democrats.

Sad to say, many of the voters of Gloucestershire have yet to reach the advanced state of consciousness that makes a 'foreigner', in their eyes, acceptable as their local MP.

And Mr Dhanda isn't doing himself any favours by getting adopted in a cathedral city in the West Country that has a 5 per cent ethnic population, most of whom are of West Indian or Gujarati origin, and very few Sikhs.

On my desk are the CVs of all the candidates shortlisted as prospective successors to Tess Kingham.

To anyone who knows Gloucester, one name leaps off the page. Janet Royall was born in Hucclecote, has lived in or near Gloucester all her life, and has an impeccable record.

I gather that moves are afoot in the party to change the nomination. All candidates have to be approved by the National Executive Committee of the Labour Party, which can simply impose an alternative candidate of their choice. They did it in neighbouring Swindon.

Alternatively, Mr Dhanda could withdraw to allow another candidate to be adopted. It will be fascinating to see how far Labour is prepared to go to hang onto its Gloucester seat.

For my part, I'm long since over being upset about Worsnip's article. But it's here because it's a part of my political race to Parliament – a hurdle myself and the people of Gloucester would have to overcome. And we did. Worsnip himself was a seasoned local political hack, a part of the local Gloucester furniture for decades, a respected citizen and, I'm told, a left-leaning person. It just goes to show what you can be up against in life.

PARMJIT DHANDA

I am eternally grateful to the people of Gloucester for proving him wrong at the election, and to a local party who were left somewhat bemused and angry at their local newspaper. The editor's excuse was that he was away the day the copy was agreed – but he never took the opportunity to apologise for it, despite his obvious discomfort at having to print several days' worth of letters from angry readers who were mostly unknown to me.

I must mention and thank Matt Carter – at that time, the new, young south-west regional director of the Labour Party (he would one day become general secretary). After Kate's call, my first conversation was with him. He'd popped out of the office to the supermarket to get some milk when I rang his mobile. Kate had faxed me the article and Matt asked me to read it out to him. He is an unflappable guy, so it was quite refreshing to hear the shock in his voice at just how bad he thought the article was.

Matt knew what had happened – indeed, he was the one who had sat me down a couple of days after my selection to show me how extraordinary my achievement had been, including the size of victory (I had led from the opening round and my lead had increased in every subsequent round). His level of determination to put things right made me realise how important it was to many people working for the party that I did get elected. By taking personal control of the situation, he ensured that our response was proportionate and clear and he shielded me from as much of the fallout as he could. Also, as a man of colour, there is something quite refreshing about seeing white people getting angrier over issues pertaining to your race than you personally are.

Things would get worse for me, though. Worsnip wasn't the only one who had it in for me, and if it hadn't been for Matt's support a few months later, I might well have walked away from the candidature and given Worsnip what he wanted.

CHAPTER 19

HAULED OVER THE COALS

MATT CARTER ADVISED that the best way to put the Hugh Worsnip furore behind us was to just concentrate on bread-and-butter issues. I needed to become Mr Gloucester. They had identified that my people skills on the doorstep were extremely strong and wanted them deployed to white working-class areas in particular to reassure them that I was not the axe-wielding foreigner I was painted out to be.

Being easily identifiable made my brand strong. I was seen at the rugby regularly, not in the posh seats but standing in 'the Shed'. As the only brown face among thousands of white locals, I got noticed – but the welcome was surprisingly warm. My regular attendance even got written up in *Shed Head*, the popular local rugby fanzine. I was soon finding unexpected Labour support in hidden quarters. It wasn't long before the call from the boardroom came asking if they could host me before a big match. It became an open invitation, although they understood why I preferred to pay for my own ticket and stand in the Shed rather than be seen in the club's executive boxes too often. I felt a bit sorry for my Tory opponent – a nice local lad who'd been coming to the rugby all his life – standing in the Shed and barely being noticed. Having said that, not being noticed when you go about your business can have its advantages in life.

With Rupi and Zac at Gloucester City Football Club

As a west London boy, I needed to occasionally trade the big match days of Gloucester rugby, with crowds exceeding 10,000 at Kingsholm, for my true love – football. It was a bit of a secret love because the two sports didn't always rub along favourably. My presence at Meadow Park helped swell the numbers at Gloucester City Football Club to a modest two or three hundred. A strong and abiding affinity began with the club. They loved the fact that I liked coming even though it obviously wasn't to meet hordes of people. I enjoyed the relative solitude and the opportunity to let my guard down. I wasn't on show there.

I was running campaigns too. I formed a human barrier across a road with residents to raise the issue of heavy goods vehicles going through residential areas. I also stood outside a supermarket collecting names for my petition to ensure that money from the sale of local land went back into funding a kids' play area.

People *really* wanted to meet me. If nothing else, the offending article had spiked interest in me, although the number of elderly white women who would tell me I was 'just like their grandson' never failed to bewilder me. 'Hmm, my dear,' I would say. 'Is your grandson 6 ft 3 too? Is he wrapped in brown skin and does he have an exotic name?' No. But he was just like me nonetheless, which was nice.

The name thing was interesting too. Gloucester developed very many variations on Parmjit. With a lovely rolling of the 'rrrr's, it often became 'Parrr-mit' – for some reason, the 'j' would frequently go missing. I would one day realise that, although he was from Glasgow, House of Commons Speaker Michael Martin would have the 'j' problem too whenever he called me to speak. The other Gloucester variation to my name was 'Parrrm-jairt', with the 'jairt' sounding like an elongated 'jet' plane. But it was very charming.

I resisted all attempts to try to have my name changed to a more acceptable Anglo-Saxon nickname that would make me more palatable on the ballot paper. I am who I am. In fact, on one occasion I went to the other extreme and reverted to Punjabi roots.

I was actually in enemy territory – in the local council ward of the guy who was standing against me for the Tories. The blue-rinse brigade seemed to be fascinated by me and I was soon holding court with a delightful group of Tory ladies. That wasn't my conclusion but just what they had declared to me: 'You're from that London, aren't you?' I could see one of the Tory gents in the background smirking when she said that. She continued, 'Ooh, I used to live there in the 1960s.' The conversation soon turned to my unusual name. There were four lovely staunch Tory women around me now, all chipping in:

'What's your name? I can't remember it.'

'Is it Indian?'

'No, Vera. I heard it is Pakistani.'

'My friend told me it's from Uganda!'

'Ladies, please don't quarrel over me!' They giggled. I could see that around the room I wasn't really winning friends among the card-carrying Tory Party members at the Kingsholm YMCA. *What's he doing in our territory?* I was having fun, though. 'It is an Indian name. My mum told me what it meant once. Shall I whisper it to you?'

'Ooh, yes, please. Tell me, tell us.'

'I can't.'

'Oh, you said you would. Go on…'

'Well, Parm is related to the Punjabi word *piyar*, which means love…'

'Ah, Ethel. Did you hear that? His name means love! How beautiful.'

I hadn't finished. '…and *jit* means to win. So Parmjit means 'winner of love'. But you won't tell anyone, will you?'

'Oh, bless, he reminds me of my grandson!'

So anyway, I was making inroads, obeying Matt Carter's instructions and working with my local party to get out there and win with love – or should I say with *piyar*. But there was trouble at t'mill. And it was coming from above – inside the Labour Party.

· · ·

I was summoned to Millbank Tower in December 2000 and told that the general secretary would like to see me. Margaret McDonagh was her name (now Baroness McDonagh). She thrived on having a tough, even fearsome reputation. Despite having worked for the party I'd never had much to do with her. I obviously wasn't one of her favourites because she never had much to do with me and never gave me as much as a glimmer of a smile, but that wasn't a problem – the vast majority of us were in the same boat.

I actually have a reasonable and courteous relationship with her these days, but back then I had more than a feeling I was not on her A-list. I was soon to realise that, if I had made it to W, X or Y in her alphabet, then I was still doing better than expected.

When you run a big organisation, and particularly if you're relatively young and a woman, being tough and assertive may well be the best way of making sure you get the respect you need. There are no two ways about it: Margaret was good at her job. But it's a close line between being aggressive and going over the top. When I look back now to my personal diary account of that day at Millbank Tower, and the conversation with Margaret, the level of anger I was left seething with still jumps off the page. And so does the hurt.

I was twenty-nine, starting out a long way from home, repairing and rebuilding a party. I was, at times, very lonely and full of self-doubt, with the pressures of holding on to one of the country's most politically pivotal seats on my shoulders. The volunteers were great but I had no employed staff unlike other key-seat candidates. It was an unusual situation to have a marginal-seat MP standing down. As well as being the PPC, I found myself taking up the role of MP on political issues. A chemical plant in Tewkesbury had been responsible for an explosion and a toxic gas cloud that threatened the wider area. I took up the issue with John Prescott, who was very helpful to me on the matter, and I ended up clashing with Tess, who didn't want to damage her relationship with Laurence Robertson, the Tory MP for Tewkesbury. But the explosion affected Gloucester too, and Kevin's view as leader of the city council was that we should intervene. So I did.

These kinds of things caused tensions, as did the Home Office's plans to disperse 500 asylum seekers to Gloucester a few weeks before polling day. I wasn't an opposition candidate so I had to engage in the politics as well as build the party – and take hits from the people who wanted me to just smile and kiss babies. Then there was the local newspaper and its medieval views about 'foreigners' from London.

All this aside, we were doing really well; I just needed to feel supported by my party's establishment. I had hoped this meeting with Margaret would be arm-around-my-shoulder time. It was pretty darn far from that.

If Matt Carter was making me feel like an asset at the regional office, then the meeting with Margaret McDonagh left me feeling like I had no right to be there and that it was a disaster for Labour that I had been selected.

Looking back, that may well have just been Margaret's style; her way of firing me up to make sure I won. And it did fire me up. Perhaps beginning the meeting by telling me that she knew I must have been surprised to win the selection in a seat like this – 'certainly this time around anyway' – wasn't the best way to start with me. It felt pretty clear that she had a view of who should have been the candidate – and I wouldn't have made her longlist.

I may not have helped the situation by responding to her rather than just taking my medicine. But I did feel she needed to be reminded I'd done the Euros in 1999 and performed well. I was no apprentice. Furthermore, if she had looked at the number of local nominations in the process, she would have known I was in the running to win the selection.

Margaret decided to focus on my 'laziness' and 'arrogance' instead. I sat and took it. I suspected this was partly meant to be a motivational lecture, although the motivation bit was somewhat lacking. There also appeared to be a bit of unburdening about Millbank's failure to stop me in my tracks.

Perhaps in her mind I was still someone who had slipped through the net – a Trot from Stoke Rochford Hall.

There was another person in the room with us, occasionally taking notes. Carol Linforth. She looked uncomfortable, forlorn even.

I like her – at the time I think she was head of the elections unit. Her eyes were mostly turned away as I went through my leathering and her face looked a bit like a parent watching their partner going over the top telling off a child, wanting to say something, or possibly intervene, but not wanting to undermine them – or perhaps, in this case, not having the authority to do so. I don't know.

You can't doubt Margaret McDonagh's record as a general secretary, so perhaps she was right to handle the situation the way she did.

I don't know how p–ed off I was at the time, but my written recollection was that I was in the mood to jack it in that evening. *Let them have the candidate they want and they can explain it to the media.* Even if I was hurt and upset, I don't think I was ever quite that stupid.

That night I had to journey through slush and snow to Swindon for a regional fundraiser. Matt Carter asked me how the meeting had gone and I told him. I told him I knew that the bosses didn't want me and that I'd had enough.

He listened and told me it was OK. I'd had my bellyache to him and he understood, but he needed me to draw a line under it. He was going to do everything he could to make sure we would win, including getting me an organiser to work in the constituency and support me. Between him and my friends in the trade union movement, we put together a package to fund the employment of someone Matt had hand-picked.

Theo Bertram would become core to what we needed to do. He would also tell me whenever Carol Linforth from Margaret McDonagh's office called:

'What did she want?'

'She wanted to check you were on message at that event you spoke at.'

'What did you tell her?'

'I told her you were. In fact, my problem is I can't ever get you *off* bloody message.'

CHAPTER 20

WHEN ELSIE MET TONY

IT WAS SATURDAY 26 May 2001, less than a fortnight to polling day, and yet another big day in my life (they were coming thick and fast now). It was the business end of the 2001 general election campaign, so Tony Blair was coming to Gloucester to make an election pledge about coach travel for pensioners.

I had met Tony just a few times before. The first time was at 10 Downing Street in 1997 at a garden party for staff as a thank you for helping deliver the landslide victory. I'd never been to Downing Street before and the whole thing was rather overwhelming. When I rocked up next to him in the garden I rather timidly asked him to autograph my invitation card – which he did. I took it home to show my parents that night. Dad cried when he saw it: 'When I came to this country I never would have believed one of my kids would visit Downing Street and meet the Prime Minister.'

Return to Downing Street, 2002, with Rupi

Well, today the Prime Minister was coming to meet me in the constituency I was on course to represent in Parliament. This wasn't lost on my parents, who joined hundreds of Gloucester residents in the Barton Olympus Theatre, awaiting Tony Blair's arrival. As the sun shone, a large group of us walked to the theatre carrying balloons and leaflets. Cars tooted, photographers and TV cameras descended, and a crowd built up outside the theatre. It had the mood of an election. Being a key seat, the billboards were festooned with political posters. We walked past a couple on the way – one depicting William Hague morphing into Margaret Thatcher and another in the style of a movie poster. It was a spoof: 'Economic

Disaster 2' featuring Hague and Portillo. OK, not sophisticated stuff from us, but it was meat and drink to election campaigns.

Labour's national poll lead was solid as we were defending a 179-seat majority, but we took nothing for granted. My diary had literally been bursting at the seams for months. The daily rounds of canvassing voters, visiting school gates, attending luncheon clubs, speaking at hustings meetings and dealing with the media made my head spin. The media were taking a particular interest in me. I was seen as quite symbolic of 21st-century politics, but if I lost this seat you could bet that it would be goodbye to any BME candidates in white areas in the future – no other CLP would take a gamble like mine had again. Protesters gathered by the crash barriers outside the theatre to sing: 'Tony Blair, shame on you, shame on you for turning blue!' But just as vociferous were the Labour flag-wavers singing (less imaginatively): 'We love you, To-ny!'

I entered the theatre and saw it was packed. The party's media machine was very organised so, as you'd expect, all of the networks and major newspapers were there. Sky was broadcasting live and the party had its own TV crew who had been with us all day out canvassing in Coney Hill. The Prime Minister's every move this close to polling day was carefully followed – scope for good and bad news. Margaret McDonagh and her team were there in person, probably to keep an eye on me in case I called for a workers' uprising against capitalism.

Margaret asked me to announce to the audience that there'd be a short delay, asking me to not make it sound like Tony had had a fatal accident en route. I had actually worked that out for myself, but was obviously very grateful for the advice. The audience gave me a rapturous round of applause just for coming on to the stage. *If only politics were always so easy.* More applause after I said Tony was going to be late. Instead of the Prime Minister, they then got a singer called Jane McDonald from *The Cruise.* I'd never heard of her but the pensioners were enthralled. Half an hour later she was still filling in for the PM. She did some Dusty Springfield and some Cilla Black and I was worried the audience would be disappointed when she had to make way for the main event. But it was 2.30 p.m. and I still hadn't seen Tony, so the show had to go on. I was getting anxious. It was now my role to welcome everyone to the New Olympus Theatre and present Paul McKenna. *Paul McKenna, the hypnotist?* I'd had no idea he was going to be there. The audience lapped it up, although he didn't hypnotise anyone – it would have been a good opportunity to try out hypnotism in a marginal seat – he just went on about how great Tony was. Then he finished and we had to bring Jane McDonald on again to fill more time. By this time I was really starting to worry that either Tony wasn't going to make it or folk would see him as an anti-climax because they were enraptured by Jane.

Dad came over to greet me at the back of the theatre. 'You OK, son?'

I must have seemed a bit nervous and distracted. 'Just waiting for Tony, Dad. He's quite late.'

'Oh, he's here.'

'No he's not, Dad – he's late.'

'I just saw him.'

'What? You just saw Tony Blair? Where?'

'In the toilets. We had a chat.'

'What? What do you mean?' This was all a bit much. Parents are great, but they can sometimes do things to embarrass you, like telling your future boss what you were like as a kid. I took a deep breath. 'What did you say to the Prime Minister, Dad?'

'I'd been to the toilet. He was doing his hair in front of the mirror. I told him I'm Parmjit's dad.'

Sounded fair enough. Jane McDonald was still wowing Gloucester's pensioners in the background.

'Dad, did Tony Blair say anything to you?'

'Yeah. He said, "I'm Tony Blair." Then I gave him a hug.'

'You hugged the Prime Minister? In the toilets of the Barton Olympus Theatre?'

'Well ... yes, son.'

At least he didn't show him any pictures of me as a kid or tell him I'd voted for John Prescott as leader. I hope he didn't, anyway. Then suddenly the crowd erupted as Tony walked on stage with a giant bouquet of flowers for Jane McDonald.

He delivered a passionate speech and made his pledge for subsidised travel for pensioners. He paid glowing praise to me and no doubt Mum and Dad were in tears again, but that's what parents do. The fact that this was all happening while I sat there, under the light beam of a Sky News camera, seemed unimaginably strange. This was the Prime Minister. This was a general election. After finishing his speech and soaking up the applause, Tony was led to the bar area to be greeted by a group of us.

The first thing he said to me was: 'Hello, Parmjit. I met your dad in the toilets.'

'Yes ... I heard.'

'Great guy.'

Say what you want about Tony Blair – and people usually do – but his people skills and his memory are something special. When we'd run into each other in the lobbies in future, he'd often ask after my dad. Or I'd pre-empt him by saying: 'My old man sends his best.'

'Ah, great guy.'

It was a bit of a running joke at home. Tony's people skills were so acute that when our eldest boy Zac was born on 1 January 2006, he sent a lovely handwritten note. A few days later, Cherie was doing a private visit to Barnardo's in Gloucester and I went with her. Afterwards she had tea and cake with party activists and saw pics of newborn Zac. She must have gone back and mentioned it to her husband because the next day a second congratulatory note arrived from him – so we had to find another frame to put that one in. You can say perhaps he didn't even remember writing the first letter, but that wasn't the point. I wasn't that bothered about handwritten notes because I'm more cynical than most about the sincerity of politicians, but Rupi was really pleased. It made a difference to her. So, when Max was born three years later and there were no notes from Gordon Brown to frame, she was livid about it because her eldest boy had two! Silly things of little consequence – but, at the same time, silly things that can make a difference to the people you live and work with. Anyhow, back to the Olympus Theatre…

The bar area had been selected for a photo opportunity and interviews with a group of ten pensioners. Between Tony and me sat Elsie Hedge in the beautiful old theatre bar. Elsie was one of

our stalwarts. Her stern look and silver hair made her look like a
Tory but she'd been head teacher of one of the local schools and
had done a stint as a Labour councillor. She sat with me, her parliamentary candidate, to her right, and Tony, her Prime Minister,
to her left and had the nation's television cameras and photographers at her feet. They were all there – Sky, BBC and ITV – at
ankle-level, looking up our nostrils.

Elsie turned to the Prime Minister: 'So, do you remember 1979?'

'I'm sorry?' said Tony.

She leaned closer to him. With all these camera lights trained
down on us, the pensioners were too intimidated and polite to
have private conversations. Plus, let's face it, if the Prime Minister
is sat a couple of paces away you're likely to let him lead the conversation – and nobody knew where this conversation was headed.

'1979,' she pressed.

Tony looked across at me with that slightly raised eyebrow
thing. For all he knew, Elsie might have actually thought she was
in 1979. I kind of nodded to him. A nod cannot always get across
a message as complex as 'She's not senile, she's actually very sharp,
but she's playing a game with you because she's got a crafty sense
of humour'. Whether my nod expressed anything to Tony or not,
with the phalanx of media at his feet it was best that he had a go
at engaging with her.

'Yes, I, err, remember it pretty well. I think.'

'No,' she chipped in with her stern headmistress voice. 'Do you
remember the 1979 general election? You wrote to me.'

I could sense a bit of relief on his face. The conversation had
some context, but I doubt if in that moment he'd quite twigged

where it was headed. 'Did I really?' he replied, and then added something about what he was doing in law at the time.

'That's right,' said Elsie. 'You wrote to me seeking the nomination to be Gloucester's parliamentary candidate. I've still got the letter, you know.'

The realisation on his face was a picture. Rather than deny it, he smiled and nodded. 'I did, you know. That's right.'

Then Elsie concluded: 'Yes, but we decided we had too many lawyers from London to choose from that year. But you've done well anyway.'

. . .

As an aside, in 2003 I was given the honour of seconding Her Majesty's Loyal Address (the Queen's speech). Tony Blair returned to Elsie Hedge's theme when he responded to my speech in the House of Commons. Here's a snippet from Hansard, November 2003:

> *Prime Minister (Tony Blair)*: As I am sure the whole House would agree, my Hon. Friend the Member for Gloucester (Mr Dhanda) also made an effective and amusing speech. I am particularly grateful that he did not remind me that before I entered the House I was rejected as the Labour candidate for Gloucester; obviously his qualities are far more appealing both to the party and to the electors there. The Gloucester seat was, as he explained, the first seat for which my Hon. Friend had applied, and, as he said rather movingly in his tribute to his constituency, the people of Gloucester showed, by sending

him to the House, that all they cared about was his character, his commitment and his talent, and that is an example to all.

As for Elsie Hedge, a former mayor of Gloucester, she lived to the age of ninety-one before dying peacefully in hospital in March 2006. I had the privilege of again telling the tale of her conversation with the Prime Minister at her funeral service at St John's Church, Gloucester.

CHAPTER 21

WHAT VICTORY
LOOKS LIKE

WHEN YOU ARE a PPC for a general election campaign the lines in your life can become very blurred. My 2001 general election campaign was a mishmash of every aspect of my life: class, race, faith, home, work, family, friends, party, personal. It's hard to compartmentalise the different aspects of your life when the date for a general election has been set. All your worlds collide as people from every part of your existence descend upon you for polling day and its run-up. People have different motivations for wanting to help during an election. For some, it is curiosity about this intriguing political world you are about to enter; for others, it's a burning desire to see you succeed. For the party faithful, it's about changing the world; for the people you went to university with, it's a great opportunity to get drunk and party in a new venue. I was just grateful for the help, regardless of motivation.

I decided I could do very little to keep all of these compartments of my life segregated so I just let them collide in Gloucester and tried to be relaxed about it. It culminated in polling day – 6 June 2001. Rather than fret about all these people meeting each other, talking to each other and learning things about me, I figured I already had enough to fret about so I let them all come together, socialise together, work together and share embarrassing stories about me together. Part of the joy of this election, and the subsequent ones I fought in the city, was the clashing and combining of different universes. It was truly diversity in action – a reflection of my life, where I had come from and the wide variety of people I had journeyed with. Because of an outbreak of foot-and-mouth disease, the expected polling day had been put back from May to June by the Prime Minister. By the time he actually visited the palace to call the election, we were all chomping at the bit to get cracking and get on with it.

Kay Mills, my agent, was superb at handling the groups of visitors, whatever their size, cultures or needs. She would make them feel included and she got them contributing to the campaign, often abetted by my mother. I would let Kay know who, to the best of my ability, was coming and she would organise the rest. It typically happened like this:

'Kay, a group of my councillor friends from Hillingdon want to come down to campaign.'

'Lovely! When?'

'Tomorrow.'

'Oh … nice … how many?'

'About a dozen, I think. And they would like to stay over. And they like Indian food…'

'OK. I'll make some phone calls.'

Kay and the team would then have some sandwiches, tea and biscuits ready for their arrival, before putting them to work out on the doorsteps around the city. We'd all meet back at the party offices and go out to eat or Harjit Gill, the local postmaster, would arrange for the Gloucestershire Asian community to organise a mini banquet for our troops. On a rota they would come in to supply us with curry or pizzas or chicken and chips. We would then decamp to the England's Glory to tell tales of the day's campaigning and, as my worlds collided, have a joke or two at my expense. Kay would then ensure that our visitors were dispersed to local party members' homes for the night.

Other regular visitors included members, activists and fellow staff from my union, Connect. They were so helpful you could have been forgiven for thinking they were trying to move me on from my career in the union movement to Parliament as quickly as possible. Coming out to canvass in the shadow of Gloucester Cathedral was a very different experience for a crowd mostly schooled in urban London politics. They had not seen this level of intensity in campaigning before: people locked horns over each vote; Cabinet and shadow Cabinet ministers came pouring into the area every other day; the parties were carpet-bombing voters with direct mail.

Gloucester campaign leaflet 2001

But the urban sophistication of those extra pairs of hands was warmly welcomed by Labour Gloucestrians. Trade unionists love a cause and they had really adopted this one – with even greater gusto following the Worsnip article. The younger trade unionists I worked with would usually stay at my flat with me. Spare room, sofas, a spot of carpet – it was all up for grabs.

The visitors poured in. Family members came from across the country – male and female; young and old; cousins, uncles and aunts (with varying English language skills). Everyone wanted to be involved. Some of my uncles wore turbans, which was a strange sight for some Gloucester folk. In this inclusive campaign they were given the choice of whether they wanted to knock on doors, deliver leaflets, stuff envelopes, ring voters or sit at polling stations on election day. Members of the Black Elders, students, the Malayalee community, the mosques, the gay and lesbian associations – and even the blue-rinse Tories I'd met – all waded in to help.

And when my university friends decided to roll up, not all of whom were of my political hue, they too were put to work. One of them turned up at the party offices on polling day after a three-day drinking binge. Vince is a great mate, but a total liability at times. We all know someone like him – great person, but can't stay out of trouble. I understand he turned up at the T&G not smelling great and said: 'I'm not feeling good, and don't really support the Labour Party. But if my mate becomes an MP today I want to be here for the celebrations afterwards. Could I have the keys to his flat and get some sleep until polls close?'

Theo didn't know what to do with him as Vince curled up in a ball and fell asleep at the party offices.

But my mother knew how to deal with him. She gently nudged him awake with a kick in the ribs and said: 'Vince, time for work, not sleep!' She dragged him to the toilets and told him to wash his face under a tap. It wasn't a multiple-choice question, so he did it. Before he knew it, he was clean (or at least cleaner), sobered-up, frog-marched to a car and driven to a polling station to take numbers in Quedgeley for four hours. There was to be no slacking in this campaign. People played hard, but they worked even harder.

A few days before polling day, as people were beginning to flag, I requested some assistance and reinforcements from my old manor. I let Kay know that some of my councillor friends from Ealing would be coming down to help gee us up. A minibus of councillors arrived at our offices in Gloucester. I'd been their agent and organised their election in 1998, so now fifteen of them had arrived to return the favour. Kay got them organised with leaflets and they delivered to two wards in one afternoon.

The campaign had gone very well. We'd worked solidly from the day I was selected and, as the masses descended on Gloucester for polling day, I was satisfied we were on the cusp of something special.

I had shut out many distractions from my life. From being a political outsider I now found myself courted by party high command as they pushed my name for media documentaries and candidate profiles. I think the penny was finally starting to drop that I was not the kind of person who would let go of the ball. I did profile pieces, at the party's request, for Channel 4, *The Observer* and ITV, who were doing a more in-depth feature on one candidate from each party. I was reluctant because I just wanted to concentrate on the campaign, but the Labour Party needed me. They knew how short they were of ethnic minority candidates and they had one now – a capable one, with a working-class back-story, who was on the verge of winning in Gloucester of all places.

Polling day felt like a good day. Matt Carter's appointment of Theo proved to be an inspired one. Over the months he had really helped us get the party machine ticking smoothly. The local author-ity nearly mucked things up on the big day by failing to open one of the strongest Labour polling stations until nearly 9 a.m. (by law polling stations must open at 7 a.m.), but I had just plugged away with a team of activists in the 'Dhanda-mobile', geeing up activists and linking up with teams around the constituency all day to knock on hundreds of doors. I tried not to think about anything other than the next doorstep, the next conversation. I didn't dare think of any-thing else. I knew I would have to deal with whatever came after 10 p.m. – when or if it came. My only sighting of my Tory oppo-nent during that day was as our people carrier pulled up alongside an old blue agricultural Land Rover. Its megaphone spouted 'Vote

Gloucester born and bred!' and a giant Union Jack was unfurled through its roof. It looked and sounded like an image of the past.

You can never have enough helpers on polling day, but we were well served with a local party of 300 members augmented by neighbouring constituencies and a wider network from all over the land. We worked hard until we dropped at 10 p.m.

Belinda, my brother's wife, then took me back to my flat, where I showered, shaved and put on a fresh suit and red tie. Belinda made me some tea and I waited in the flat, watching the exit polls. They predicted a Labour landslide. I was now in the hands of my agent Kay, our organiser Theo and their team of activists, who were all monitoring the votes at the count at Beaufort School. They had charged my brother with the responsibility of ringing me every so often to tell me how it was going. Members, activists, relatives and friends had started congregating at the Irish club, relaxing and kicking off the all-night election party that would culminate in my arrival after the count (either as the defeated candidate or the victorious new MP).

As the minutes and hours ticked by, Budgie rang me but told me nothing. All he would say was it was nip and tuck – too close to call. I was getting frustrated and said to him that I hoped he wasn't trying to manage my expectations. I had seen the exit polls and I knew we should be winning. But he persisted: it was too close. We were either a few votes ahead or we were slightly behind. Waiting was tortuous. *Could it really be that close?* Perhaps Hugh Worsnip was right all along.

Eventually, after 1 a.m., Budgie rang to say that Belinda should bring me down to Beaufort School. The count was coming to a conclusion but it was still unclear if I had won or lost.

So I made a conscious decision – my fate was sealed either way. I was just going to go down there and finish things off with a smile, come what may. And, in any case, with all my pent-up adrenalin it would be good to just get out of the flat. Belinda drove us to the count. It was quite funny because she had no idea where she was going. It was pitch dark and I was too distracted by the news on the radio to be aware of my bearings. How ironic that I should get lost tonight, after getting lost on my arrival in the city a year before. Luckily there was a map in the glove compartment.

I made sure I had a skip in my step. They say politicians are frustrated actors – that's true. On nights like that one I really needed my acting skills. Seeing so many tired and sweaty people made me feel comparatively fresh. I made a point of visiting every one of my party members in the hall to have a joke with them, thank them, hug them or kiss them. Win or lose, they had given everything to the cause. Paul James looked particularly tired. He had been there from the beginning and looked like he had personally counted every vote. His face was red and sweaty and his suit looked lived-in. Paul is a decent person and whether he was going to win or lose that night I felt that his colleagues, who were well meaning, needed to look after him as well as mine were looking after me. I hope they did.

Still beaming and smiling, I went over to Mum and Dad. I was always more worried for them at these occasions than I ever was for myself, so I needed to exude confidence. They were OK, but apparently it had been very close and they had been very worried indeed.

Whether by design or incompetence, someone in the RO's team had decided to hold back the bundles of votes cast in Barton & Tredworth, Labour's strongest ward. Around the time I arrived, these votes were added to the two piles and the votes were no longer neck and neck. As I talked to Labour colleagues I could sense camera lenses and TV cameras training on me. I knew the national narrative of the night, having spent hours holed up watching on TV, and I was conscious that every smile, every pat on a shoulder, every hug or shake of the head could end up being broadcast. But I was also growing more comfortable with it. Our people looked more relaxed; the opposition's people looked more dejected.

Paul James's agent, councillor Phil Awford, came over, wanting to take me aside for a chat. I was a bit wary and could sense Labour eyes on me in case it was going to kick off. There was no reason why it would've, but tensions run high at these events.

We shook hands and he said: 'I just wanted to tell you I think you fought the most brilliant campaign.' I could see he meant it. Then he added: 'Spare a thought for my guy; I've had to pick him up off the floor tonight. He thought he was going to win.'

And I did. Although I felt young and indestructible, it was a reminder of the old political saying, 'All political careers end in defeat' – and I would not defy gravity for ever in this marginal seat.

It was nearly time. A local radio reporter asked me to do an interview and wasn't prepared to wait for the outcome: 'Let's do this as if you have just become MP.' I declined. She persisted because she wanted to be first out of the blocks with the news. But there was no way I was going to tempt fate by doing that so I left her frustrated.

Kay and I were then led into a huddle with the other candidates and agents. There wasn't much fuss. We nodded and everyone accepted the result. The ranks of supporters and counting agents looked to us for confirmation, but other than nods and smiles we refrained from giving any. My political race had spanned a generation, from the farmlands of the Punjab to the hospital floors of the NHS in London. There had been political pick-axes to dodge along the way in an unconventional journey to the heart of British democracy. A few more minutes wouldn't hurt.

We stood on the podium and mayor Terry Haines read out the result. Labour had won with a majority of 3,880. After the eruption of noise and emotion from our people I took the microphone. I hadn't dared to prepare an acceptance speech but I had a fair idea of what I needed to say. It was a time to be gracious, not a time to talk about whether my grandfather was in Dunkirk, whether we had disproved the racists who thought Worsnip was right or whether I should have been 'Gloucester born and bred'. I simply thanked and congratulated everyone and talked about the future. I promised to be a 'heart and soul' MP for Gloucester. This place had given me an opportunity and I was determined to return the favour by making it a better place for all those who had voted for me and those who had not.

At the count with Theo and my brother

With my agent Kay

Victory speech   *Election night 2001, with Mum and Dad*

There's nothing like looking at the people you love when they're happy. The rest is a bit of a blur. I remember posing for a picture with my parents, a really nice one that Spencer Feaney, the *Citizen*'s editor, gave to me as a peace offering. I also remember really wanting to get to the Irish club to see my friends, but before I could leave Beaufort School there were a couple of things I had to do. The chief executive handed me an envelope with the words 'City Member' written on them. It was the itinerary of the mayor's diary for the coming months. I have no idea to this day why I needed it but I like to think it was part of an ancient tradition. I doubt it, but I didn't have time to ask. My phone was whirring with activity. Word was getting out. Some callers didn't know and wanted to enquire about what was happening. Others wanted to leave messages to congratulate me. So, before Budgie could bundle me into his car, I wanted a moment alone to change my voicemail. I spoke into my mouthpiece: 'Hello, this is Parmjit Dhanda, Member of Parliament for Gloucester. I can't take your call right now, but if you leave me a message I'll get back to you.'

It was just me and my big brother for ten minutes in the car to the Irish club.

'So, bruv,' I enquired, 'good night?'

'It was OK. For a Thursday.'

He smiled and we laughed. My brother can be a very serious guy but it was nice to laugh with him, at the end of a mad day. But he soon brought it back to serious matters.

It was a useful opportunity to start mapping out the future. The Labour majority had more than halved so I needed to hit the ground running with a well-equipped constituency team of staff getting on top of the casework as soon as possible. Budgie was very impressed by Theo. He was a talent but he wanted to move to London. It would be good to keep his skills in the team as he knew the constituency well now and it was important to start building for re-election in 2005. They say that if a new MP has a good first six months, people remember them, but if you have a bad first six months, you rarely recover.

The car arrived at its destination and in the wing mirror I could see three Asian men in a huddle, hugging each other; two men with turbans, one without – my two chachas (Dad's brothers) and my dad. How I would've loved to be a fly on the car park wall in that quiet corner then. The Irish club car park on the night of the 2001 general election was a long way from their village in India. There had been many fights and arguments between them about who knows what over the years, but tonight they were close, they were emotional and they looked like they couldn't quite believe what was happening. They were together.

The Irish club was a wall of noise, singing and unrelenting joy for many hours. My speech to the Labour faithful and my friends was upstaged by my mother's words. They gave her a big bouquet of flowers and she took the handheld mic to say thank you. I had never heard her speak to a public gathering before, and I haven't since, but she was utterly nerveless. As well as thanking them for all they had done and talking about how proud she was that night, she asked them to take care of her son.

It wasn't an easy act for me to follow but it was an easy audience for me to please that night. I remember looking around at them all. What a strange journey: my family with my new Gloucester Labour family; young keen activists; sage old party hands; people I hadn't seen for years; gatecrashers who wanted to be part of the night; university friends; work colleagues – a wonderful tapestry of people. I hadn't won; *they* had. And it made me feel good.

CHAPTER 22

ARRIVAL

SOME HABITS ARE hard to break. I went through a phase of listening to loud gangsta rap in the 1990s – bands like NWA and artists like Ice-T. In June 2001 I still had the tapes and CDs in my car. I rolled up at the carriage gates of the House of Commons in my little red car on my first day at work and lowered my window. As I did so, a black security guard came up to me and asked, 'Can I help you, sir?'

Unfortunately, NWA may still have been blaring from my speaker system with words about what they would like to do to the police and others in authority. 'I'm the new MP for Gloucester, sir. Elected last Thursday. Just reporting for work.'

The security man cracked a smile a mile wide. 'No way, mister! Give me five!'

And so I did.

I went through security checks – they looked under the bonnet of my car – and then I parked a few feet from Big Ben before going in to find out about my new workplace. There was a cloakroom to leave my coat and bag. My name was on a coat hanger. The hangers were all in alphabetical order. Mine was between Dobson (Frank) and Denham (John). The coat hanger had a pink ribbon on it. The pink ribbon was to hang my sword on. I don't have a sword but, when I told them about the pink ribbon, my nephews bought me a *Star Wars* light sabre. Within weeks, though, the door keepers were ordered to do a sweep of the cloakroom to remove MPs' toy swords and my light sabre was never seen again.

My first day heralded my first opportunity to get a proper sight of the House of Commons chamber – I had spent remarkably little time in my life in Parliament.

It was early and it was quiet. One of the door keepers let me in around the back of the Speaker's chair. I'd mugged up on the place and knew that the two red lines on the floor in front of the benches were two full light sabres apart to keep the Empire and the Rebels apart in the event of another Clone War. I saw the wooden 'fence' where MPs could sit whether they were in government or opposition and I knew that was where the phrase 'on the fence' had originated. I saw the bag behind the Speaker's chair, where I would spend much time organising and then depositing petitions in the years ahead on behalf of the people of Gloucester. My eyes were caught by the glint of the despatch boxes, leaned on by prime ministers and leaders of the opposition for so many generations – Lloyd George, Asquith, Churchill, Thatcher and Blair, to name but a few. Little did I know that one day I'd be destined to lean on those despatch boxes myself as one of Her Majesty's ministers – the first Sikh to do so.

As a minister at the despatch box

But today my interest in the despatch boxes was due to the fact I was to swear in as an MP in a few hours' time. Swearing in involved standing by the Speaker, as he sat in his chair, and either affirming loyalty to Parliament or swearing an oath of allegiance to the Queen with your hand on a holy book of your faith (if you had one). The despatch boxes, I had been told, contained the holy books of all major faiths (Jedi is not a faith).

I may not have been representative of any of the great faiths of Gloucester – there are only a small handful of Sikhs there – but I was very conscious of the importance of faith to the thousands of church- and mosque-goers in my constituency. As well as Bibles and Qurans, the boxes held the Gutka – part of the Guru Granth Sahib, the Sikh holy book. I'm not someone who would ever proselytise, and I say each to their own when it comes to religion, but it would be a big moment for me and my family when I swore the oath with our holy book in my hand.

The lure of the despatch boxes was strong. I was all alone in the chamber and couldn't resist the opportunity to get a bit closer, maybe even have a little lean on them.

Suddenly the silence of the chamber was broken by one of the door keepers. I was startled. He asked me who I was and where I thought I was going. I took the little green and white badge out of my pocket and everything was OK. I can recall for a moment I really wanted to quote Eddie Murphy in a film called *48 Hrs*. I wanted to say, 'I am your worst nightmare. I am a black man with a badge.' I paraphrase – that's not exactly what he said – but you get the gist.

In fairness to the door keepers, they have a job to do and they do it very well. He was very apologetic and embarrassed and was always good to me after. Perhaps that day was a useful education for us both.

CHAPTER 23

'I'LL BET HIS GRANDFATHER WASN'T AT DUNKIRK!'

SOMETHING HAPPENED IN the 2001 general election that I wanted to try to put right, at least in some small way, if I were to be lucky enough to get elected. Well, as you know, I got elected. So let me tell you a little about what had so rankled with me. It's to do with a remark that got under my skin.

If you're a political anorak, you'll recall Oliver Letwin saying something daft. Let me narrow that down a bit for you: if you're a political anorak you'll remember Oliver Letwin saying something daft during the 2001 general election campaign about £20 billion of unannounced spending cuts that the Tories would secretly implement.

He was swiftly slapped down by party leader William Hague and went into hiding. So when Hague and his Tory battle bus came into the Gloucester docks for a campaign stop, the sages at Labour high command had printed off Oliver Letwin masks for our activists to wear as they took on the role of welcoming committee for the Tory leader.

It's all part of the fun and frolics that goes on at election time. Quite rightly, I was kept well away from it as the young and innocent candidate, but many a story of the day was recounted to me by my activists who laid a very mild and Middle England-style siege to the Tory battle bus in their Oliver Letwin masks.

Put off by twenty Oliver Letwins (who wouldn't be?), I gather Hague barely stepped off the bus before he was on his way to the next key marginal. But among the high jinks came an unsavoury moment when a Tory councillor (whom I won't name) blurted out some choice words about yours truly to the Labour activists, including: 'I'll bet your candidate's grandfather wasn't at Dunkirk!'

The 2001 general election campaign in Gloucester was already shrouded by the racial undertones of the 'A Right Royall Mistake' article in the *Gloucester Citizen*. And the Tory slogan, adopted on their local literature and posters, was urging folk to 'Vote Gloucester born and bred'. Very hard to manage a trick like that if your parents are from northern India.

During my time as Gloucester's MP, my paternal grandfather

passed away. In his advancing years he could only make one trip to Gloucester, but it lives long in my memory. He sat quietly with a whisky in the corner of the civil service club, my grandmother beside him. An upright and sturdy soldier, with a turban, a long white beard and a smart suit, there was something quite magisterial about this exotic visitor. He knew it and he kind of lapped it up, as if all the celebrations going on around him to mark our victory at the general election were actually a tribute to his genes. As Labour Party members and inquisitive Gloucester revellers went to engage my grandparents in their dozen words of English (they lived in Southall, where Punjabi is the local language), he occasionally nodded his head approvingly, had his glass refilled and even managed to get an offer to have his portrait painted, although I don't think he knew it.

The local branch of the legion latched onto his story and he became a bit of a local folk hero. Swaran Singh Dhanda had fought in the Second World War in the Indian Army. Replete with turban and beard, he was part of the Royal Bengal Engineers, serving King and country in the Commonwealth's forces in Burma fighting the Japanese. As a result, the Burma Star Regiment of Gloucester had a soft spot for our 'papa', as he was known, and de facto for me too. It still surprises me how little the wider public know about the Sikh contribution to the Allied war effort.

The 'I'll bet his grandfather wasn't at Dunkirk' remark really did rankle with me. I didn't mind people having a pop at me – it was part of my job – but give me a break and keep my family out of it, especially if you don't know your war history, mate. I became ever more determined to put the record straight during the 2001 election campaign – if only I could get myself elected.

Quite soon after the election, an opportunity was to arise.

The 2001 Labour Party conference was a celebratory affair marking the 160-seat majority we had just achieved in the election in June. But it was a bizarre conference. The sobering events of the Twin Towers in New York City on 9/11 happened just three weeks before our party conference and they were fresh in everybody's minds.

As I sat in a packed Brighton conference hall, soaking up a weird feeling of celebration tinged with the mourning of global slaughter and the onset of a war, a familiar voice courted my attention. It was my own voice. That was weird. The giant screen was running one of those musical montages designed to whip the hall up. You know the kind of thing: cheers around the hall as text flashes across the screen saying: *Independence for the bank of England! More doctors, nurses and hospitals! Lower taxes and free ice cream!* That kind of thing.

Then there was footage from the campaign in Gloucester that I'd forgotten was ever taken, or assumed would appear in a training video on 'How to knock on doors in the pouring rain', gathering dust on a shelf at head office. The footage showed me walking through a street in Coney Hill, flanked by party members handing out leaflets and posters. I was talking about the importance of 'connecting with working-class communities who had voted Labour all their lives – now it's our turn to show them they matter to us if we want to retain their trust'. I was giving high-fives to kids on the Coney Hill estate as they whizzed around on their BMXs. They probably actually just wanted me to get out of the road but the footage looked good anyway. The moment passed and I felt quite pleased with myself before the video moved on to Blair and Brown arriving at Birmingham New Street station to the sound of Heather Small singing 'Proud' as they headed to the manifesto launch.

Then it was back to me again. This time it was footage from Tony Blair's visit to Gloucester's Olympus Theatre. I'm the first to confess I can be a jammy sod sometimes; I'd found just the right words to encapsulate the moment and mood in the packed Brighton conference centre. I looked up at myself on the big screen as it zoomed in on the rosette on my lapel. 'We've had the Prime Minister here with us today. It's been a long day today, a tiring day and an exhilarating one. But I tell you this: there's nothing I'd rather be doing.' Cue footage of a Parmjit Dhanda poster going up in somebody's window and the words on the screen fading in: *Parmjit Dhanda, on June 6th, was elected Labour MP for Gloucester.* The cheers went up around the hall and I knew I had arrived. Conference now knew who I was and everyone from the Chief Whip to delegates from around the country was making their way over to pat me on the back.

I enjoyed the moment. I knew I would have a big future ahead of me and I was likely to be one of the belles of the ball. But even then I couldn't hide from the cynic inside me that knew it couldn't last forever. While I was riding this wave I needed to use it to do some good things. A testing motion was about to come before the conference, moved by a hero of mine – the black general secretary of the TGWU, Bill Morris. Before I had even left my seat I could see out of the corner of my eye party officials huddled, looking my way, contemplating how to deal with this awkward motion and how best to tap into their new weapon. But I had a plan of my own – one that my grandfather would be proud of.

Motions at conference were something New Labour got very het up over. The leadership wanted to win every debate, crush every rebellion and demonstrate cast-iron unity to the British public. So, when Bill Morris, the union movement and some left-wing delegates moved a 'composite resolution' suggesting that 9/11 was being used by some employers as an excuse to sack people just because they could – rather than as a consequence of 9/11-related economic uncertainty – the leadership wanted the motion killed off. As their shiniest new weapon, I was asked to wield the sword from the podium of the Labour Party conference. But I'd never spoken at conference before and Bill Morris was, and is, one of my heroes.

Although high-risk, I figured the canniest thing to do was accept the challenge, take to the podium and find the right wording to unite the party and gently get the motion dropped. Simples.

Well, that was a sleepless night. When I was called to the podium I still wasn't totally settled on what I was going to say, so I did what I felt always worked best – I spoke from the heart. In fairness, it was relatively easy after I began by introducing myself as 'Parmjit Dhanda, since June of *this* year the *new* Member of Parliament for Gloucester.'

I nearly got a standing ovation for that alone. Not, I think, because of what we had achieved, but because of the realisation that I didn't look like what a Member of Parliament was meant to look like – and I particularly didn't look like what an MP for Gloucester should look like in their minds. I was barely thirty, I wasn't white and I wasn't a Tory.

I played on this for a moment and served a cold dish for the *Gloucester Citizen* (I knew some of their journalists were glued to the TV at the time): 'They said the people of Gloucester weren't ready to accept a "foreigner" as their local MP!' I let the howls and hisses for the paper die down a bit by standing back and giving a shrug. 'Well, conference, here I am…'

For a Labour audience bred on a life's diet of equality and the fight against racism, that was manna from heaven and cause for celebration. It was a special moment in my life after the crap I'd gone through thanks to the pen of Hugh Worsnip and I had to laugh, though I urged the audience not to encourage me. We were all relaxed now so I could make my serious point in the short time allotted.

The mood of the western world at that time, just days after 9/11, was a mood of anger. Thousands had been slaughtered and most people felt it was time for retribution, so the argument I was going to make wasn't to be a fashionable one.

One of the first people to suffer the retribution post-9/11 had been a Sikh shopkeeper in the US. He was murdered because he had a turban and a beard, and therefore – to the uninitiated, the angry or the downright stupid – he must have been a sympathiser of Osama Bin Laden.

I talked about my grandfather. He wasn't at Dunkirk. But I made the point that he and hundreds like him had served King and country alongside British forces in the Sikh regiments in Burma. Many of them had laid down their lives for this cause. Surely people like my granddad had earned the right to walk our streets without fear of insult or intimidation?

The resolution was dropped and a compromised form of wording was agreed that day. I also made my grandfather a happier chap – and others like him too, I hope.

Swaran Singh Dhanda passed away in November 2004 a few months after my grandmother. I worked with the Ministry of Defence to run the 'We Were There' exhibitions in shopping centres around the country (including Gloucester), where we honoured the memory of individuals from different backgrounds and communities and their contribution to the war effort. So something good did come from William Hague's visit to the Gloucester docks.

My grandfather Sarwan Singh Dhanda, 1966

CHAPTER 24

NOT JUST A
PRETTY FACE

I T'S QUITE A nice problem to have: because you're different –
i.e. you didn't go to private school, you didn't attend Oxbridge,
you're not overweight, you're not over the age of fifty and you're
not white – you find yourself in demand as a politician. This is
ironic given not being all of the above often holds you back from
getting into politics in the first place.

I say it's a nice problem, but it is still a problem. There was no
shortage of glitzy party invites, media opportunities or attractive

women looking for an angle for a meeting with me about conjured-up policies. Fortunately, I had good people around me keeping my feet nailed to the floor. A bit too firmly at times.

Within my first month in office I had received a random offer of marriage from India via airmail and a charming letter and CV from a 'friend' of a minor celeb suggesting we should consider hooking up. I didn't reply to either. It wasn't long before I was *Elle* magazine's 'It boy' of the month (although I must confess I never really worked out what an 'It boy' was, which in itself means I was poorly qualified for the role). My staff limited my attendance at Asian awards ceremonies to once every two months (there seemed to be one every week) and after a while we started being a bit more discerning about what media I was and was not going to do.

In the early days it was 'yes' to everything. I loved doing it. After starting out presenting the newspaper review on Channel East all those years ago in front of an audience of three people, I had become comfortable and easy on camera. But I needed to become more disciplined and not spread myself too thin. The more you do, the more you're asked to do, and I needed to learn to say no. My media in-tray of requests looked something like this:

- Radio 5 live PMQs programme: Yes.

- BBC Asian Network Kabaddi on the radio at 7 a.m. on a Saturday morning: No. OK, then – only once a month.

- *Richard & Judy*: Yes.

- Andrew Neil, BBC *Politics*: Yes. But do your homework first.

- Local and regional media: Yes. As a priority.

- Ethnic minority TV station I've never heard of: Definitely not. Until Mum tells me she occasionally watches it and I'm betraying my roots if I don't do it.

You see, these were difficult decisions to take and in my first term I did a lot. Too much. There was a fair bit of 'eligible bachelor' stuff kicking about and it started to get out of control when the local newspaper and regional ITV station picked up on it. The lady from ITV broadcast a piece roaming around my local Asda in Gloucester with cuttings from magazines that had placed me in various positions on their hit parade of most eligible young men in the country. She went up to the check-out ladies and talked to one who I recognised – I'd bought a value pack of Pot Noodle from her till just the previous weekend. The interviewer basically said: 'Well, what do you reckon?'

'Yeah, not bad. Bit of a sort, ain't he?'

OK, it was funny, and an ego rub for me, but not what I would want to be remembered for. I didn't want to become a figure of fun – and it also made my life a bit awkward shopping for groceries in Asda. In any case, I don't think politicians do 'cool' very well, and they shouldn't even try to.

I learnt that lesson one day after I had completed a really good live interview on *Richard & Judy* about the creation of Police Community Support Officers. I'd said what a good thing they were and Richard tried to challenge me with something like: 'Isn't it just policing on the cheap?!' I calmly replied that it wasn't; it was about additional resources for a more visible presence on the street. He said: 'Oh, yeah, good point.' And then Judy patted me on the hand to say how lovely it all was. Hardly Jeremy Paxman.

I was seeing Rupi by then and when I got home she was very excited. 'Wasn't it great?' she said.

'Thanks. Thought I did well.'

'No, silly. Liv Tyler was on before you. She's brilliant!'

'Oh. Who's Liv Tyler?'

'Don't you know anything? She's a really famous actress. She's the daughter of the guy from Aerosmith and she's going to be in *Lord of the Rings*.'

Rupi had recorded my interview for me and she rewound to the 'far more interesting' Liv Tyler bit. I said: 'I recognise her. She was sat next to me in make-up. She did mention something about films but I had no idea who she was.'

'You … idiot! She's really famous! You sat next to her and didn't know who she was? I wouldn't vote for you if you told me that!'

I knew that this cool new world was one in which I needed to be a bit cautious. My team in 2001 – David, Tricia, Helen and Theo – were also aware that we had big opportunities in terms of my profile, but it had to be used for one end: making a difference to peoples' lives in Gloucester. We were conscious that I couldn't become just a pretty face commenting on the world around me. I wanted to change the world. *We* wanted to change the world. And we were determined Gloucester was going to reap the benefits of that change.

CHAPTER 25

LEAVING MY MARK

GLOUCESTER HAD SUFFERED from a lack of investment for over a generation. Its economy had shrunk while neighbouring Cheltenham had become a popular tourism destination in the heart of the Cotswolds. Its public services were in terminal decline too: the hospital was a decaying tower block; higher education had left the city; further education was soon to leave to consolidate in a single site in Cheltenham. The historic mills in the docks had been long since abandoned and all that was left was rusting away. The docks themselves were barren. For a generation they had started and stopped building work on a major road scheme (which was known locally as 'the road to nowhere'). It was meant to be the South West Bypass – a road that would open up the city from north to south, joining the growing suburb of Quedgeley on its southern end to the city centre, the docks and the ring road – but the money had run out and it was going nowhere. Meanwhile, the former cattle-market site in the north of the city was like a lunar landscape – its planning applications kept getting knocked back. While the housing register of people in need was growing hand over fist, these major developments to the north, centre and south of the city had all stalled.

Many of the school buildings I visited were crumbling, and secondary education was caught in a trap whereby four grammar schools in the city creamed off academic talent from the wealthy Shire whilst the local kids were sent on journeys to outlying comprehensives that had become de facto secondary moderns. The political battles in the Shire hall lurched from all-out attempts to close grammar schools by some in the Labour group (although without a legal framework to do so from Westminster) to all-out opposition to innovation in the comprehensive sector from the Conservatives (who tried to maintain the purity of the grammar schools at huge detriment to the others).

The influence of the well-heeled Shire – or 'Cotswold Cavalry' as they were known locally – had balkanised public services that should have been in the areas of greatest need (i.e. my new constituency) to areas where they were not needed as much. The police headquarters, for example, was in a poor-quality building in Cheltenham – an area of high land value – whereas it needed to be in a fit-for-purpose building in Gloucester – where the bulk of intensive policing took place.

There had been some progress. Tess had worked with the Health

Secretary Frank Dobson to initiate the £35 million rebuild of the hospital and Kevin, as council leader, had managed to get the last of the major lottery grants for a brand new leisure centre. But again and again I would hear the voices of locals stating: 'Nothing ever happens in Gloucester.'

The public realm was in need of a real overhaul and I would have plenty of work to do. But I was young and aggressive and determined not to let anyone stand in my way. I was in politics to deliver change and I was going to unlock the floodgates, however attritional the process would be. I was going to use the weight of my friends in the government to help me achieve it – whether they liked it or not. Rapid change and new investment would make me a lightning conductor and the Gloucestershire Tories would hate me. I wasn't interested in being a fluffy MP who just popped along to fêtes and kissed babies. This was about power, and I would use it to deliver for people who had been left behind in a city that was in the slow lane.

. . .

I didn't make all of the changes that happened in Gloucester between 2001 and 2010 myself – there were many people involved. Kevin Stephens and councillors of all hues had a vision for the docks and other regeneration sites, but they needed someone who could stir it up and make things happen. And that was where I came in. Pretty soon I was lobbying hard for £18 million for the missing chunk of the road to nowhere. David Jamieson was the very helpful Transport Minister I cut a deal with. He said: 'If we give you

£12 million, the council should be able to wrangle the other £6 million from private developers.' That sounded reasonable to me so we shook on it, the road deal was agreed and it has now been built.

The people of Hucclecote had problems with their noisy neighbour the M5. Hucclecote needed a noise bund (a barrier) between the road and the houses. With a little more help from the Transport Department, aided by a public meeting and a petition, we got some noise abatement measures put in. But we hadn't finished with the department yet. There were no signs to Gloucester from the M4 and officials weren't prepared to budge and put some in. However, the ever-helpful Mr Jamieson asked me about the precise location I wanted the signage and then agreed to get them put in. Gloucester was now officially on the map, signed from the M4 for the first time.

The hospital rebuild was going well, but it was always a bit short of money or in need of some more funds for operating theatres. But I intervened with ministers whenever they needed me to keep things on track and, when it was complete, I got the Secretary of State John Reid to top off the job by coming to open the restored Gloucestershire Royal Hospital.

When the constabulary was a few million quid short of building the new police HQ Gloucester so badly needed, I went to see the Policing Minister and the funding gap was plugged.

I opened an £18 million campus that brought university status to the city and I relentlessly badgered John Prescott and his junior ministers to get the long-awaited decisions on thousands of homes at Quedgeley and the Cattle Market moving. It happened, and building work began on homes and a retail park.

Regeneration and doing deals became my stock-in-trade.

David and Tricia managed my Friday night surgeries where I dealt with the more practical stuff – the drains, the neighbourhood disputes, the immigration cases – but I was really at my best delivering on the big stuff.

So many pieces started falling into place around the city chess board, and yet the biggest piece eluded me. It was the one I had promised to make a difference to on the night I was selected – the Gloucester docks.

. . .

On paper there was a £1 billion regeneration project taking shape that would involve the public and private sector working together to build new retail, restaurants, hotels and education facilities, creating 2,000 jobs along the Sharpness Canal basin. British Waterways (BW) owned the land in the docks and had got into bed with Peel Holdings, the developers of the Arndale Centre in Manchester. They wanted to build a £280 million factory outlet in the docks – in other words, one of those modern shopping centres, a bit like Bicester Village, full of units holding big brands selling last year's fashion lines at discounted prices. Sounded cool to me, but the council – now under Tory rule – was flaky about this patch of land, which had remained barren for generations. They were worried that new shops in the docks might damage the shops in the town centre. I understood the pressure they were under but, for me, this was about ambition for the city. Surely the offer of a mini Bicester-style shopping centre was different to what other shops were offering? And, in any case, part of the deal needed to be about better walkways and links from the city centre to the docks to benefit more shoppers and present a bigger offer of restaurants, bars and a new evening economy. But, as the council stalled on making any firm commitment, I could see everything slipping away.

The other complicating issue was that I had taken the principal of Gloucestershire College (Greg Smith) to meet Alan Johnson in a last-ditch attempt to keep further education studies in the city. The old college was dilapidated and set to shut for good. Greg and I made a pitch to Johnson, who was then the Higher Education Minister, for what amounted to the biggest grant ever from the government for a brand new college – also to be located in the heart of the docks. We sold Alan the vision of the new shopping centre, the footfall from the college on the opposite bank of the Sharpness Canal and the new bridge linking the two, as well as the wider regeneration of the docks, including homes, a hotel and leisure facilities. It was ambitious but doable, and Alan liked it, so the Learning and Skills Council agreed the funding – but only if we got planning permission and started building within a few months, or else we'd lose the money.

I spent the subsequent weeks trying to blackmail – for want of a better word – BW into handing over the land so we could build the college. But they wouldn't agree to the college putting in a planning permission request on their land unless it was tied into the same planning application for the shopping centre. Through early day motions (EDMs), questions in the House and leverage on the minister Alun Michael, I tried to get BW to allow us to press ahead with this much-needed college before we lost out on the funding. But they wouldn't budge unless they were guaranteed planning permission for their chums at Peel to build the shopping centre.

Things came to a head when Rupi and I were on holiday in Spain in the summer of 2004. I got several panic-stricken messages that there would be no college, no shopping centre and no regeneration of Gloucester unless I managed to sort out a deal within the next month. I couldn't leave this in the hands of councillors or anyone else any more: the project had become centred around me as the 'can do' man. I was investing a lot of time and political capital in this scheme and was desperate to make it work. Plus the money was set to go back to the government coffers very soon because of a lack of progress.

The problem with government these days is that all parties have created a state where former public bodies like BW have been encouraged to become so commercial that you can't force them to do something in the public interest any more. All you can do is use your powers of persuasion as best you can.

With my legs dangling in a Spanish swimming pool and having spent over an hour on the telephone to minister Alun Michael for the second time that day – I was desperately trying to get him to ensure BW would see sense rather than just pitch their wagon at Peel Holdings – we finally fudged a partial solution.

Alun and I agreed a date for a meeting upon my return. Alun would lean on the BW chair and chief executive to attend. It would be in John Prescott's office, with Prescott's personal private secretary taking notes of the meeting to add formality. Present there would be the leadership of the city and county councils, senior representatives from the Regional Development Agency, English Partnerships (the agency involved in land deals) and Peel Holdings, and the college principal Greg Smith. I would chair the meeting and that would be it. One last crack – regeneration for Gloucester or bust.

Upon my return, and the return of Parliament, the meeting took place. I had hoped Alun Michael would be able to join us but he had his hands full that day as the minister with responsibility for banning fox hunting (the vote coincided with the day of our meeting – 15 September 2004). The meeting began at 4 p.m. and we could hear the semi-riot taking place in Parliament Square from the top-floor conference room at Defra in Smith Square. As I sat them all down I joked that this process had been no less arduous than trying to ban fox hunting. We did intros and everybody around the giant boardroom table was impeccably well behaved. I let them all talk about their issues with the proposed regeneration scheme. Jem Williamson, Greg's deputy at the college, talked about 'phasing', which in other words meant: 'Please let us build the college now or we lose it forever. Don't use us as a tool to make the council give you planning permission for your shopping centre before you give us the land we need.' We all understood the hidden meaning.

BW and English Partnerships talked about the 'funding gap', or in other words: 'Where's the cash for all this going to come from?' I told them I was confident a combination of the pledge from the government department for the new college and the land sale from the existing college site would be bankable. As long as I looked confident and assertive I realised people weren't going to press me on just how precarious all of this was. I saw this as a once-in-a-lifetime opportunity and I wasn't going to let them walk away because we might be a few million short. I could deal with that problem later.

Then BW and the city council raised 'planning issues'. Again it was all very civil, but from BW we knew this essentially meant: 'Give us planning permission for our £280 million shopping centre before we hand over land for a college, you buggers. We can't trust you and we think you'll turn down the shopping centre as soon as you've got what you want.' The council's perspective was: 'Oh, we don't really know. This is such a big decision. Some people might not like it. Can we just put it to one side for a few more years, please?' I paraphrase and exaggerate slightly, but I hope this helps you understand where we were at.

Very helpfully, the RDA chipped in with some figures: £2.5 million for the site and £5 million for the bridge (£1 million of which the RDA would put in). It was all doable.

But as time ticked by, nothing had been settled. The problem was still there and we had no compromise. So I summed up everybody's position and said it was time to walk away. Then I said, 'Or how about this for a proposal?':

> British Waterways hands over the land for the new £32 million
> FE college to be built. Peel Holdings and British Waterways
> agree to decouple the college from their planning application
> for the retail centre. However, the city council fast-tracks the
> application for the retail centre.

The city council chief executive has stated that an application could be heard within two months, but such a big decision would mean the full council undergoing training to vote on the scheme, as it would be too much pressure for just the councillors on the planning committee. But it can be done within two months of this day.

Next, the local urban regeneration company, the college and the RDA shall all make submissions in support of the application. [None of which I had cleared in advance but I was cobbling this together on the hoof. All of those agencies were present and they nodded as I said it. This really was the last-chance saloon for them now anyway.]

And finally, I will personally write to the council and publicly state my support for their planning application for the shopping centre, as the city's MP.

It all went quiet.

I waited for an answer from BW and, more importantly, Peel, who were calling the shots. Lindsey Ashleworth of Peel looked at his MD sat next to him. Then he looked at me and said: 'Go on then, we'll take a punt.'

Silence again and a large measure of disbelief in the boardroom. Before anyone could change their mind I said, 'Thank you. That is agreed, then.' I turned to John Prescott's private secretary next and asked, 'Have you got that minuted?'

He nodded.

I looked at my watch: *4.57 p.m.*

The Gloucester docks had lain barren for over a generation.

After fifty-seven minutes locked in a room together, we had cracked the deal to unlock their potential.

Done deal – the regeneration of the docks. With Greg Smith.

CHAPTER 26

ASSISTING ENGLAND'S ASSISTANT MANAGER

I N THE SUMMER of 2002 the country was going World Cup crazy. Parliament was no different. My first major league piece of opportunism as an MP was to follow up David Beckham's injury-time equaliser against Greece at Old Trafford (which earned England the point they needed to qualify for the World Cup) with an EDM.

An EDM is just a few sentences an MP strings together, hands into the Table Office and then, hey presto, it goes out into the public domain. Other MPs then weigh in by adding their name in support of this crucial parliamentary instrument (or piece of worthless parliamentary confetti – depending on your viewpoint).

I came up with a plan to catch the public mood by tabling this motion first thing on Monday morning – the first working day after England's win – before any other MP got round to it. October 2001, EDM 211 states: 'That this House congratulates David Beckham's England team on their qualification for the 2002 World Cup and calls on Her Majesty's government to do all in its power to ensure that the World Cup finals are shown live on terrestrial television.'

Perhaps there was a threat to World Cup games being shown on terrestrial television at the time, or maybe that was just an added piece of opportunism by me at the time. I hope not, but I can't actually remember.

I sat down at PMQs with a copy of my motion in hand and sent it down the Labour benches like a *psst – pass this on* message. Up and down the lines of benches it went, coming back to me within minutes with, hey presto, eighty-four MP signatures on it.

From a very early stage in my career I was aware that I needed to take care of myself physically. Despite the marginal nature of my seat, I hoped I was bedding in for a career of a decent length – although with late-night votes, a stressful day job and the constant scrutiny you're under, it's small wonder MPs have a shorter life expectancy than society at large – and therefore I decided I needed to get into good habits from the outset.

So I joined the gym at Millbank and also played football – I even played a few games for the UK parliamentary team. Despite the fact I've never been the most talented player, I do love the game.

And that's where I met Lawrie. Lawrie McMenemy is, to this day, the most successful football manager in the history of South-ampton Football Club. He won the FA Cup with them in the 1970s and had managed players like Kevin Keegan and Mick Channon during his career.

Lawrie – for some reason I've never been able to work out – was manager of the parliamentary team at the time. Goodness knows what he made of a bunch of unhealthy MPs plodding around the pitch after having worked with players like Keegan and Channon. A sense of humour must've helped, and he's one of the funniest people I've ever known in my life, as well as one of the nicest. Come the 2002 World Cup, Lawrie managed the parliamentary team on its ten-day tour of Japan, where we played matches, raised some money to help rebuild the national stadium of Afghanistan and watched England's opening games against Sweden and Argentina.

One night I was at a dinner with Lawrie and members of the team as he regaled us with stories about his time as England's assis-tant manager, alongside Graham Taylor. They worked together in the ill-fated 1992 European Championships, when the team's failure to make it past the group stage led to the infamous *Sun* headline: 'Swedes 2 – Turnips 1.'

If that wasn't bad enough, it was followed a couple of years later by the *Do I Not Like That* fly-on-the-wall documentary that tracked Taylor's team as they failed to qualify for the 1994 World Cup. Lawrie, despite his 6 ft 4 frame and stature of a former Coldstream guard (because he was one), very cleverly managed to keep a low profile through the documentary while his boss ranted like a madman about 'not liking orange' when Holland

(and Norway, oh, and arguably San Marino) put the sword to a ragged England side.

To come through such an ordeal with his dignity intact only enhances my admiration for Lawrie –although, as a coach, I shall never forgive him for substituting me after twenty minutes in the Olympic Stadium in Tokyo after I missed a sitter against the Japanese Parliament. To this day I don't understand what he meant as he bawled at me during throw-ins to 'Switch it! Switch it!' I don't know what 'switch it' means and I never got to grips with his string theory for defending – 'Imagine there's a piece of string running through you, from left back to right back!' – when I was moved from the forward line to full back. I'll bet the Brazilians don't tell their back four to think of themselves as a piece of string. But then again, he's won the FA Cup, and I haven't.

Back to the story now and the conversation over dinner in Tokyo…

Lawrie was telling us about the 1992 Euros and what it was like to take an England side to a major tournament. I could recall, as a football anorak, the pre-tournament crisis England had with their right backs. Days before the tournament, England lost their first- and second-choice right backs to injury. I think it was Lee Dixon of Arsenal and Phil Bardsley of QPR. Anyway, it is customary to replace an injured player with another player to cover the same position, but – for some reason I (and probably many other football fans) did not understand – Graham Taylor's England called up a player named Keith Curle. He was a talented player, but a central defender, not a right back.

If you're about to become an international player and deliver success at a major tournament, then why not sign a new boot deal? I believe that's what Keith Curle did – and who could blame him? (Although turning up in new shoes may not be the best preparation for playing against some of the best footballers in the world.) So Lawrie and Graham Taylor found themselves playing a classy French team in the opening game of the tournament with a third-choice right back, who was not in his natural position, being skinned alive by a skilful and quick French winger. However shiny his shoes were, something needed to be done urgently.

Luckily a solution was at hand for Lawrie and Taylor. The ever-dependable Leeds United left back Tony Dorigo was sitting on the bench. Tony Dorigo is one of the most underrated footballers ever to play for England – great going forward, excellent at taking free kicks and comfortable in possession of the ball. Unfortunately for him, he was rarely in possession of an England shirt because Stuart Pearce was even better than him.

As Lawrie described this key moment in his career, I felt his pain. It was a bad tournament for England but, from my recollection, we'd managed a goalless draw against the French. So it wasn't that bad, was it? However, I didn't recall Dorigo at right back. Hadn't the midfielder David Batty been drafted into that position? It had caused some ridicule in the media at the time. Lawrie nodded. Apparently, despite all those years warming the bench as cover for Stuart Pearce, Dorigo didn't fancy coming on at right back that day so they had to find another solution. Come on, Dorigo – how hard can it be? Just think of a piece of string!

'Lawrie,' I said. 'Why didn't you play Dorigo at left back?'

Lawrie looked at me with the kind of disdain he usually saved for when I was missing sitters in the Olympic Stadium. 'Pearce was left back. He's world class. We needed a right back!'

'But Lawrie,' I protested. 'Pearce [or "Psycho", as he was affectionately known] would run through walls for his country. Why didn't you just switch him to right back and let Dorigo come on in his natural position?'

I watched Lawrie McMenemy ponder this for a moment. It was as if his brain was engaged in the footballing equivalent of calculus. This old footballing maestro (did I tell you he won the FA Cup with Southampton?) took a moment and, after a very long pause indeed, said: 'Aye, Parmjit. That could have worked. But I didnae have your mobile phone number in 1992.'

CHAPTER 27

MPS AGOG – WAS IT ONE FINGER OR TWO?

BONFIRE NIGHT 2002 and the Tory Party was almost ablaze. Iain Duncan Smith (IDS), their leader (yes, he really was, you didn't imagine it), announced that his party must 'unite or die'. The latest split was over gay adoption. IDS was trying to whip his party up to oppose it and Michael Portillo led the rebellion against him on Bonfire Night. So, what was front-page news the next day? What was everyone talking about in Parliament afterwards? It was the Duke of Edinburgh, what he'd said to me, what I'd said to him; whether he'd patted me on the back or whether he'd flipped me a V-sign. Here is how *The Guardian* reported it on their front page:

ONE FINGER OR TWO?
MPS AGOG AT PRINCE'S SALUTE

The Duke of Edinburgh's gift of the gaffe left him accused yesterday of giving a V-sign to a Labour MP at a Buckingham Palace reception.

Prince Philip was said to have issued the salute after encountering the backbencher at a party for parliamentarians hosted by the Queen.

According to a prominent Labour MP, the famously prickly Prince raised his fingers then turned on his heels after an exchange with Gloucester MP Parmjit Dhanda.

The Prince, on hearing Mr Dhanda had been a student and trade union official before entering the Commons, had told his guest: 'You didn't do anything then.'

Mr Dhanda, formerly assistant national negotiator in the Connect information technology union, used his industrial experience to turn the question back on the Prince. 'What did you do before becoming the Duke of Edinburgh?' he inquired. The Prince replied he had been in the Royal Navy, serving during the Second World War.

What did, or did not, happen next was the talk of the Commons bars and tearooms yesterday, with the precise details a matter of dispute.

The prominent Labour MP, who asked not to be named, swore that the 81-year-old Prince gave Mr Dhanda a V-sign. 'It was unmistakable ... bloody funny,' said the MP. 'I didn't know he had it in him.'

Mr Dhanda, attempting to laugh off Monday night's incident, said the Prince playfully raised one finger, not two.

The Blairite, elected in 2001, said: 'He didn't stick up two fingers, he pointed up one and said "There you go", patting me on the shoulder before he went. He had a big smile on his face and it was very much in a sense of fun.'

A palace spokeswoman suggested there was 'obviously not a lot going on' in the Commons if MPs were talking about whether the Prince raised one or two fingers.

'The Duke of Edinburgh would certainly have no intention of making a gesture of that nature in Buckingham Palace or anywhere else to a member of the public, let alone an MP,' she said.

The Prince is no stranger to controversy and his comments have a habit of backfiring. Trying to share a joke this year with a blind woman and her guide dog in Exeter, he said: 'Do you know they have eating dogs for the anorexic now?'

As I hid in my office for the coming days, avoiding calls from journalists and colleagues alike, virtually every newspaper covered the story – from the *Daily Mail* to *Corriere Della Sera* in Italy, from *Private Eye to* a Bolivian publication that I could not pronounce … and beyond.

They couldn't get enough of it and I guess I was the lucky one – since the Duke is always making gaffes, he copped the flak. Reruns of every politically incorrect statement he's ever made were reprinted – and, my goodness, there are a lot of them. But this one was a bit special for the gaffe collectors. It involved a young MP (you'll note from *The Guardian*'s coverage I've gone from being called a Trotskyite in my political life to a Blairite) and it involved the trade unions (who had their own say on the letters pages about 'Prince Philip's disgraceful insult to the movement'). It also involved rudeness and a level of mystery because I wasn't talking about it, regardless of the barrage of requests. To this day, whenever I receive messages on my mobile I still fear it's Francis Elliott of *The Times* chasing me for a quote about what happened that night in Buckingham Palace.

In the coverage, I got away with being the quick-witted victim of the Prince's crime. For years my colleagues – particularly those with republican tendencies – dined out on this story and often added their own spin on what I said to HRH or what he said to me. I've been asked about it many times over the years – the conversation, the manner in which it was said, whether it was actually one finger or two... Did I really ask him what he did before he married the head of state?

I have always kept my own counsel and my reply to these questions would always half-jokingly be: 'You'll have to wait until I write a book!'

So here is the definitive account of what actually happened the night I visited Buckingham Palace to meet the Queen and her consort...

It's one of those invites you can't really turn down. An invite for MPs to meet the head of state in her own home (one of them, at least) was not something this Mellow Lane Comprehensive kid could ever have imagined receiving. This was *woah!* Very big.

So off I went, along with literally hundreds of MPs. I remember walking up this long staircase and waiting in line. The Queen was shaking hands with each of us as we bowed or curtsied before making our way into a grand ballroom kind of a place. I don't know what it was but it was an eye-poppingly big room steeped in splendour, with paintings and curtains you can't even buy in John Lewis. When it was my turn to shake the Queen's hand I was disappointed to see she was wearing white gloves and it was more of a parting magisterial high-five than a handshake, with no time to shoot the breeze. But I had no knowledge of etiquette or any common sense about such things so there was no point in feeling offended. It was her house, her rules.

My knowledge of protocol would change over the years as I got to meet her on several other occasions, but at this stage in my life the closest I had got to a royal event was a street party for the Silver Jubilee in 1977 on our road in Hayes. I was only six and had thoroughly enjoyed it. My sister entered the fancy dress competition as an Indian princess but so did every Indian girl on Berwick Avenue. It basically involved wearing an Indian suit, as they normally did at home, but borrowing some of Mum's make-up. The imaginative winner of the contest was an eight-year-old white boy (white people still lived down our road then) who had dressed up as an old woman by borrowing (without her knowledge) his grandmother's dress, shoes, make-up and wig. Unfortunately, with a long line of MPs behind me bursting to get in to sample the household wine, I sensed this would not be the opportunity to share my story with our Queen.

I wandered around with a perfect crystal glass in my hand, and took a sip of red wine. There were lots of people there, mostly Labour from recollection. (This may have been due to the fact the

Tories had decided to have their huge bust-up over gay adoption that evening. They must have concluded that spending an hour at Buckingham Palace wasn't as much fun as spilling their leader's blood on the carpet of the Palace of Westminster.)

I was talking to some fellow MPs when, out of the corner of my eye, I spied the Duke of Edinburgh. As relaxed as you like, he came over and joined Wayne David, Brian Sedgemore and myself. He was in a chirpy mood and, like the rest of us, was enjoying his drink. Then his attention turned to me:

'You're a bit young to be an MP, aren't you?'

'Yep, probably right.' (It was all rather playful.)

'So, you're not fresh out of school then? What did you do before you became an MP?'

'My student days weren't that many years ago, but I worked for a trade union before becoming a Member of Parliament.'

'Worked for a trade union?' The Duke had a cheeky smile on his face and then delivered his line. 'So you didn't do that much then?!'

Now I thought that was funny – nice one! – and I wanted to join in this little gag-fest with my new friend. Then something sprang to mind as the perfect retort...

An older and wiser Parmjit Dhanda would have bitten his tongue and smiled, but I was young, naive and having fun – and, from the glint in Prince Philip's eye, he was certainly having fun too. Then I said: 'So what did you do before you married the Queen?!'

Momentarily I think that caught him off guard. Was the joke over? Was I about to get sent to the Tower? No. He came back with: 'I was in the navy for fourteen years. So there!'

Unbeknown to me, one of our witnesses, Brian Sedgemore, was

one of the biggest gossips in England and the story of me and the Duke was circulating almost before he'd stopped wetting himself with laughter – which may have taken an hour in itself.

Anyway, then the 'one finger or two' controversy happened. One version of events was that he patted me on the shoulder and pointed a finger as he said 'So there!', before spinning away to entertain another group of unsuspecting parliamentarians. The other version was that he gave me a two-finger salute as he turned on his heel. Whichever version of events was true, he didn't deserve a week of articles in the media trawling through his gaffe collection.

My recollection – sorry to let the republicans down – was of two people with very little in common sharing a moment of humour and harmless sparring over a drink.

For the record: yes, it was two fingers, not one.

CHAPTER 21

1889

CHAPTER 28

IRAQ

I N THE RUN-UP to the March 2003 vote, I don't think the
Whips' Office ever really thought I would vote against the war.
I was hotly tipped for promotion and so they probably thought
I just wouldn't jeopardise that by letting my principles get in the
way of a good ministerial career. That actually suited me really
well. While colleagues were being beasted several times a day – by
a combination of their whip, the Deputy Chief Whip, the Chief
Whip, the Secretary of State for Defence, the Foreign Secretary
or even the Prime Minister himself – I was largely left alone. At
first, anyway.

In fairness, the ministers, including the Prime Minister, used their political skills to convince you of the merits of military action. The 'beasting' came from the whips.

But it wasn't as if I hadn't warned them. I maintained my support for the government's attempts to negotiate a UN resolution on military action. It was actually the party whips who had gone around in the weeks running up to this vote saying: 'Stick with us. You will get the chance to rebel before our troops go into Iraq. If you want to rebel, at least wait to see if we can get a UN resolution first.'

Two days prior to the vote I was asked to attend 10 Downing Street to meet the boss. There were half a dozen of us there, mostly loyal MPs who had articulated some concerns about where we were heading and why.

We took our seats at one end of the Cabinet table. The Cabinet room is a pretty cool place to have a meeting – and a subtle way of reminding wobbly backbenchers what they may be about to give up if they don't stay loyal.

We had a particular problem that would require a lot of political charm or arm-twisting for the government to resolve, and this was a charm day. There wasn't going to be a second UN resolution. Unfortunately, Jacques Chirac, the French President, had come out and said he would use his veto on the UN Security Council to block it regardless. I don't say 'unfortunately' because I thought he was wrong – I didn't – but because it was a tactical mistake that gave the Americans, and indeed our own government, the opportunity to 'blame the French' for killing the debate in a rather jingoistic way. Unsurprisingly, this was manna from heaven for newspapers like *The Sun* to whip up a storm against the French – as if there would have been a UN resolution if Chirac had kept schtum. No chance. But, in that finest British tradition, if you need to whip the public up into a frenzy then baiting the French is a tried and tested method.

Tony came in and we made a bit of small talk. Although, actually, I didn't. Meetings in the Cabinet room with the PM should be among the highlights of your political career, but resisting a charm offensive when the country is on the brink of war isn't fun. What didn't help was the sight of most of my colleagues – nearly all of whom had stated 'Up with this I shall not put!' on the way into the Cabinet room – now falling like dominoes to prime ministerial charm, ready to take up bayonets in Baghdad, via Paris. The truth was it wasn't just the French who would kill off this UN resolution, but many other countries too.

Alastair Campbell walked in, placed a note in front of the PM and then hovered over him. Tony put his glasses on, read it and then looked at Campbell rather quizzically.

I sensed an opportunity to break some ice. 'Hurrah!' I said. 'The second resolution has come in, we can go now!' It got a laugh. Strange things pass for humour at difficult times like this. At that moment, the only way I could have averted war would have been to take on the persona of the hypnotist from *Little Britain* and say to all present: 'Look into my eyes, my eyes, not around the eyes. You will not support a George Bush-led invasion of Iraq. You're back in the room.' Then click my fingers. The daft things that come into your mind at inappropriate times…

There was then a debate about the French, Hans Blix and the

impact on the Middle East for about twenty minutes. I listened but didn't say anything. It was fascinating to see how people's positions shifted. Then Tony zeroed in on me: 'Parmjit, what are you thinking?'

I momentarily thought of Mrs Alexander and Class 3A at Yeading Primary School, when I'd said something challenging about the Falklands War. Didn't go down too well. At least my mate Raj wasn't around this time to tell me I would get our heads kicked in.

My answer was something like this:

> Tony, I really want to be helpful. But your own whips went
> around saying at the vote a few weeks ago that the time to
> judge the government [they actually used the word 'kick']
> would be now, on the eve of a war, if we failed to get UN
> support for it. I hear what you're saying about the French,
> but I don't think we can just blame them. My position has
> been consistent. This is very difficult.

I was actually proud of the fact that we were seen as the pro-European party, and Tony had led that repositioning. I believed in the rhetoric about needing to be engaged in Europe to influence it and I was most uncomfortable, as the son of 'outsiders', with any jingoism. Even against the French.

So why did I do it? It wasn't easy – not for me, anyway.

In the year 2003, it wasn't fashionable in the Parliamentary Labour Party to be an Iraq War rebel. I was doing well – a young starlet in the party among a young dream-team intake, including Purnell, Burnham, Watson, Miliband (David), Knight and many others. Rebellion was not on my mind – I was neither disloyal nor disaffected.

By accident rather than design I sat in front of my friend the late Robin Cook the night he resigned in the chamber – the night before the vote. I knew my mind well enough to be certain I agreed with every word he said. I hadn't become a rebel – I'd stayed true to my view that Britain could not go to war without that second UN resolution. That had been the party's policy throughout – until March 2013.

The night of the vote was tortuous. I remember ringing Dad and saying, 'I just can't do this, Dad. It's wrong.' He told me to do what I thought was right. He was never keen on the war.

Then I got a call to see Tony again. I think he thought I'd come round and I admit I really didn't want to let him down. He said the government would win the vote, but he didn't want to win on the back of Tory votes. We talked about Bush and his roadmap to peace in the Middle East. Without wanting to sound stroppy I tried to find statesmanlike language to question Mr Bush's sincerity on the issue.

Before I left Tony's office I promised him I'd consider what he'd said because I genuinely respected him.

When the division bell rang, my good friend Keith Hill (the Deputy Chief Whip) waved to me and urged me to get up to head to the 'no lobby'. We were voting on the rebel amendment. I can still recall the look of disappointment on his face when I shook my head, signaling that I was going to break the cardinal rule of political collectivism and defy a three-line Labour whip. I had to pass some of my strategically positioned friends from the 2001 intake, who stood next to the entrance of the rebel lobby and implored me not to throw away my career. Others, in the 'aye lobby', laughed and patted each other on the back. It made me feel really uncomfortable. I just wanted to vote, get out and drive to my parents' house in Hayes to regroup away from all this pressure.

But as I emerged from the rebel lobby a shocked and then delighted-looking John McDonnell greeted me warmly and wanted to congratulate me as I exited. No disrespect to John, but I was in no mood to celebrate.

The 139 of us who rebelled that night all had our reasons. I felt genuinely awful. I hadn't been elected as a Labour MP to spend my time voting against my own party and when I got home that night I'm not ashamed to say I cried my eyes out. The day and the run-up to it had been a huge strain. Many of us felt like pariahs in our own party at that time.

Why did I do it, then? Because I thought the war was wrong and, in time, I feared history would prove the 139 rebels to be right.

CHAPTER 29

BREAKING BAD – WITH THE LORD CHANCELLOR

'W HAT'S HIS NAME?'
'That's Roger Mills. He's one of our stalwarts, secretary of the constituency party.'
'OK. Pass me the mic.'
The people carrier slowed down as we caught up with the Labour canvassing team. There must have been twenty of them, stretched out along the avenue, carrying bundles of leaflets, wearing bright red rosettes and 'Vote Parmjit Dhanda' stickers. A great turnout

bearing in mind it was during the day of a working week. The skies were cloudy but our mood was bright in Gloucester, April 2005, buoyed by a good first-term record to defend at the general election in a fortnight's time. My local popularity was certainly enhanced by my decision to rebel against the Iraq War.

The serenity of this picturesque housing estate in Matson was soon to be broken. The people carrier's Tannoy crackled to life with Scottish brogue: 'Vote Labour! Vote Labour in…' (muffled) '…Where are we again?'

'Matson.'

'Ah yes. Vote Labour, people of Matson. Vote for dignity in retirement for Roger Mills!'

Roger turned to meet his oncoming tormentors. 'Oi! You cheeky monkey! I mean … oh, hello Lord Chancellor.'

We got out and helped Roger pick up the leaflets that had been dropped as he had turned to face us. Charlie Falconer was in good form and a breath of fresh air in the roll call of Cabinet ministers who were daily beating a path to Gloucester's door. Some of them were precious about being asked to make themselves useful by knocking on doors. Others would do it but only after giving that 'but I am in the Cabinet, wouldn't it be better for your campaign if there was a set-piece visit around my brief?' look.

Charlie just seemed pleased to be outdoors and unleashed on the electorate.

We first met in 2001 when I was a shiny new MP and he was a junior minister with responsibility for housing development. The meeting had been arranged through Paul Clarke MP, his parliamentary private secretary, in a meeting room in Portcullis House.

'What are you, an Italian fascist?' I had barely sat down and I
looked around the room in case somebody had come in behind me
carrying a violin case containing a sawn-off shotgun. 'Black shirt
and a black jacket, that's what they wore.'

'Actually,' I replied, 'Italian fascists are big in Gloucester. We're
a big family.'

'I'm sure you are – you look the part. And I'll bet you don't get
any grief at your constituency surgeries.'

'Well, sometimes you do. But that's fine; that's when the horse's-
head-on-the-pillow routine kicks in. They don't come back after
that.'

'Hmm, I can imagine. Shire horse?'

This kind of prattled on for about ten minutes until Paul Clarke
interrupted: 'Parmjit, you have an urgent piece of business you said
you wanted to raise.'

'Ah, yes. Big planning application in my patch at St Oswald's
Park. Biggest B&Q outside of China, a care village for the elderly,
affordable housing and hundreds of jobs, minister.'

'Splendid.'

'It is. But stuck in your department, holed up in a cupboard
somewhere. Can you give someone a nudge and ask them to look
at it?'

'Consider it done.'

So knocking on doors with Charlie, Roger and our band of
activists was going to be fun. The right-hand side of the road
was a park, so our team was getting strung out a bit in their
enthusiasm to win the general election there and then in Matson. Stragglers who were larking around and getting involved

in telling yarns to constituents (namely Charlie and I) were getting left behind. Never mind. Somebody would notice that we weren't keeping up and would come back for the candidate and the Lord Chancellor, wouldn't they? We kept knocking on doors in this tough working-class part of the city. It was going well for a daytime canvass. We got to the next door in the estate and a teenage lad walked up the drive behind us. We turned to give him our warm, friendly politicians' smiles and he walked straight past us, not bothering to take his eyes off his basketball boots. Charming.

'Hiya,' I ventured. Not a word as we stood alongside him by the front door. I looked at Charlie and he shrugged. As we were about to turn and walk away, the lad shimmied up a drainpipe and up to a first-floor window. He then pulled back an open window and wriggled his body through it. We watched as his basketball boots disappeared in to the house and he was gone. We looked at each other in disbelief. It didn't look good, but you had to admire it as a feat of great athleticism. I was half tempted to applaud.

As we walked up the path Charlie said: 'What do we do now?'

'Mark it down as not in?'

'Not in? Not in? Someone is definitely in – he just climbed in through the window!'

Charlie had a point. I had an idea. My trusted PA had a duty to look out after me at times like this. 'David,' I called. 'David?' We looked down the road and could see enthusiastic canvassers, David, Roger and all, disappearing round the corner. Out of sight and sound.

I had another idea. 'OK. We'll knock on the door. Maybe he

lives there. It might be his house. Perhaps he's just left his keys in the house, so needed to climb in.'

I don't think Charlie was entirely convinced. 'Yes. Many a time I've checked my pockets and realised that I've left my keys behind. You know, the first thing that comes into my mind is I'll shimmy up the drainpipe, flip my body through a slightly ajar window and let myself in!'

This was starting to turn into an episode of *Breaking Bad* – the one where the Lord Chancellor and the local MP are left by their posse to accost someone on the Matson estate after he's broken into a property. For all I knew the house could be a crystal meth factory. Or a torture chamber full of politicians. Reluctantly we went and took turns to knock on the door. There was movement. The creak of a door handle. It was him. The teenage youth came to the door. This time he had a bike with him. We were in his way. He briefly looked up at us.

'Hi,' I said.

He said nothing.

Charlie chipped in: 'Do you vote Labour?'

'No,' he muttered. Then he brushed past us, shut the door and cycled off.

Hmm. We pondered and debated our predicament as we walked towards the road. Now what? Well, at times like these (not that this sort of thing happens very often in my life) I need to put a good and a bad column in my head. If we call the police: (1) an innocent young man could get his name besmirched for entering his own home and leaving it on his own bike; (2) a rumpus could ensue with police and myself at the heart of it – not to mention a member of the Cabinet. If we don't call the police: (1) a criminal may have gotten away with burgling somebody's home; (2) tomorrow's *Daily Mail* could feature a story about a local MP and the head of the UK's legal system watching a criminal act unfold before their very eyes and deciding to ignore it.

'Well,' I said. 'There goes another possible vote.'

'He said he doesn't vote Labour.'

'You're right! Let's call the police.'

And so we did. I have no idea what conversations were had in the police control room about the Lord Chancellor and a local MP wandering around Matson witnessing someone climb in through a window. What I do know is two police cars and a motorcycle within five minutes may have been overkill. But nonetheless it drew the attention of the Labour canvassing team.

Roger was panting. 'What happened to you two? We thought you'd been kidnapped or something. 'Ere, did you see all those police cars up the road?'

And if you're curious about the man with the basketball boots … turned out he lived there all along.

CHAPTER 30

FORCE OF NATURE – CAMPAIGNING WITH JOHN PRESCOTT

WE HAD JUST over a week of campaigning left in the 2005 general election and I was taking a breather to write letters to voters in the office. Just then, our Labour Party organiser Paul Nicholson came in and said: 'Good news – we've got a Prescott visit lined up. What do you think?'

'Fan-bloody-tastic!' I said. 'It'll go wrong, Paul – they usually do – but the punters will enjoy it, and he's never boring…'

•   •   •

The first time I ever met John Prescott was in Kent at the Labour launch of the 1999 Euro election campaign. I say 'met', though 'being in the presence of' is probably a better way of putting it. I doubt he was aware I was there or had any idea who I was. It was at a sports hall in the Medway area of Kent. They had set up elevated seating around a square platform in the centre of the hall. Myself and the other ten Labour candidates were dutifully placed in the front row of seats. John Denham, as the region's most senior MP, was compère for the show.

The Prime Minister had drawn a full house. But the Prime Minister wasn't there. Due to the flare-up in Kosovo, Tony had had to cancel at the last minute and send his deputy in place. And, my goodness, he was in a foul mood. I didn't go near him. Not many people did. We were all terrified. The speech he gave to launch the event was more than tub-thumping; there was so much thumping going on I thought he was going to break the glass lectern that was holding his written speech. Not that he looked at the speech – he just growled out everything he was going to say and did it loud. OK, we can be snobby about these things and say there wasn't much subtlety to it in Medway that day. We had plenty of your *Guardian*-reading, Radio 4 *Today* programme-listening party members who drew their breath while he turned red in the face, his hair billowing about and his fists beating the lectern to a pulp as if it were the face of a Tory who had just voted against the introduction of the national minimum wage. The Radio 4 audience looked to be lamenting the fact that they would not be able to tackle Tony Blair on the EU Habitats Directive or the merits of a Tobin tax on financial transactions. But, equally, as Prescott roared louder, I could see the more traditional earthy supporter punching the air with delight. Every time he minced a sentence in anger they willed him on to hit that imaginary Tory face on the lectern even harder. In fairness to John, he can actually do calm and subtle – but certainly not that night. We got through the Q&A and could finally leave.

But that's when the Deputy Prime Minister's mood really darkened, because he was all set to miss the train to his next engagement back in London. Labour's regional director for the south-east was one of the nicest and most softly spoken people you could ever have the pleasure of meeting. He was also looking quite hassled – and who could blame him? With the Prime Minister cancelling on him late in the day, a group of angry party members on his trail and now the logistical issue of having to get his team of candidates back to the station and, more importantly, an angry Deputy Prime Minister back to London. We were ushered to the exit to get into cars heading for the station driven by regional staff and helpful activists. I was relieved that I hadn't been asked to sit in Prescott's car. He would have no idea who I was anyway and did not look to be in the mood for small talk.

The journey to the station was manic: three cars travelling in convoy, weaving in and out of traffic along the way, desperate to get the DPM to the station on time. Frankly I wasn't concerned about getting there late – I didn't have important matters of state to attend to – but as we pulled up alongside the regional director's car in the station car park I felt for him. The car doors sprung open and it was like an episode of *The Professionals*. It was Bodie and Doyle time as we ran through the car park with the DPM to get him to the train on time. The train was on the platform preparing to leave. Someone shouted: 'Stop the train! Stop the train!' The cry echoed down the line to the youngest and fittest assistant in our team who had sprinted 30 yards ahead of everyone else. As he tried to skip up some steps the Deputy Prime Minister slipped and got mud all over his suit. I could almost hear the growl. The shout down the line changed to: 'Stop the train, it's the Deputy Prime Minister!' And by now the message had reached the platform guards. 'Stop the train, it's the Deputy Prime Minister!' they yelled along the platform. Remember, as well as being Deputy Prime Minister, John Prescott was also the Secretary of State for trains. Prescott scrambled the last 20 yards with mud on his knee. He got to the door. He got through the door. It shut behind him and his frazzled assistant. Mercifully, he was away.

Breathless and panting all the way, we headed back to the car park to regroup with Kamlesh. He'd had a tough evening but looked relieved. 'Well done, Kamlesh,' I said, in between intakes of breath.

'Thanks, Parmjit … for your support…'

'That's OK, mate. You do know that train was heading for the coast and not for London, don't you?'

. . .

My only previous interaction with John Prescott was in the 1997 election campaign when I was asked to join other party staffers to ensure he got a warm welcome at a service station outside Swindon as he stepped off his coach – the Prescott Express. What could possibly go wrong? I'm a big Prescott fan. I actually voted for him to lead the Labour Party. But something invariably went wrong each time I was outdoors in his presence. And sometimes indoors too. On this occasion in 1997 he hadn't even stepped off the coach, D:Ream's 'Things Can Only Get Better' had barely begun to be phased out by the speakers and a punter by the coach steps started on him. I couldn't hear what he was shouting but Prezza was not one to walk away from a fight, as you know. On this occasion they just rowed a bit. I thought I heard John's riposte as 'You're just an effing Tory!' Or words to that effect. He went back inside the bus and the doors shut. But in true New Labour fashion the bus moved 20 yards up the car park, stopped, the music started again, Prescott descended for the second time and a few well-placed Labour bodies kept the 'effing Tory' at bay and we carried on as if nothing had happened. Remarkable.

In 2001 he famously punched a voter. Although if a lout threw an egg at me from 2 yards away I'd like to think I'd have thrown a punch back at him too. Having said that, I was fighting my first election to become the MP for a marginal seat and it was just days from polling day, so I was worried about whether John's left hook was likely to impact on our chances of winning. So when I went out knocking on doors the next day and a burly bloke ran across the street towards me, having seen the red livery of my campaign team wandering down the road, I was somewhat perturbed. Red in the face and over-excited, he went nose to nose with me, 'I've never voted for your lot! But I thought what Prescott did yesterday was bloody great! He's got fire in his belly. Can I shake your hand and wish you luck.' Bizarre but true.

· · ·

So, back to 2005. John Prescott was back on his campaign coach and on his way to Gloucester. We stood on the site of the regeneration project that I had painstakingly put together with some help from his department. About fifty party members were there in the Gloucester docks. They held up signs with Labour's pledges on them, partly because he was notorious for forgetting them and we thought they would act as a useful prompt. We waited for the Prescott Express. And we waited. I collared Paul, the local party organiser, to ask what on earth was going on. Press, TV and members were hanging around and there was no sign of the man. Paul whispered to me, 'I think he's on the M4.'

'Good. So he's on his way then.'

'But he may be heading for the north-east.'

Sharp intake of breath. 'Paul. What on earth are you talking about, man?'

'He doesn't want to come any more.'

I looked around at the party activists, all decked out in red and excited about meeting one of their heroes. 'What the ... hell is going on, Paul?'

Paul moved closer to whisper. 'Greenpeace climbed onto the roof of his house in Hull last night. They tried to install some solar panels on to his roof. He's angry and wants to go home.'

I guess you're not supposed to start tittering like schoolboys at a time like that, but what else were we to do? When the Prescott Express eventually arrived it was parked 200 yards away, on the wrong side of the Gloucester docks. I don't know what was happening but I'm told delicate negotiations were ongoing over whether John was going to do his outdoor public address to the Labour faithful in the docks, or whether he was going to go back home to Hull.

Thankfully, John Prescott put Greenpeace to the back of his mind and emerged to a tumultuous welcome from the Labour activists. With a microphone in one hand and a red rose from Aida (one of my loyal envelope stuffers) in the other, he was ready to make noise.

He used the props our members were holding up to help him recite what Labour had achieved since 1997. His very presence meant that live broadcast media was linking the national and local Labour Party and its messages. OK, he minced his words but he generated coverage, which was a good thing for the Gloucester campaign. However, as he yelled out his core Labour message to activists, I soon realised that my role as his adornment had pitfalls as well as advantages. It was a bit like being one of those semi-clad models who hold up a placard at a boxing match which state: 'Coming up, round three.' Silent and smiling, and about half a foot taller than him, I had absolutely nothing to do. Other than smile like an idiot. We made an odd couple. As the Deputy Prime Minister ramped up his volume I loyally obeyed the party's orders and stood by his shoulder in full view of the broadcasters. My job was painfully simple. *Smile*.

He was on top form, uncaged and ready to rip Greenpeace from limb to limb should they be foolish enough to cross his path. And as the words left his mouth, exhorting the activists, so did some spit. Spit landed on my lapel. To be precise, it landed on my rosette. My lovely red rosette said 'Vote Parmjit Dhanda' on it. And now it had Deputy Prime Minister saliva dripping down it. I continued to smile for the camera. Not daring to wipe the phlegm from my lapel while they were filming. He then did interviews about Greenpeace and his house in Hull. It turned out that the Greenpeace stunt had involved a group of men climbing onto the roof of his house in the middle of the night whilst his wife was at home alone. So his anxiety was actually very understandable.

Still fixed by his side, I gained some publicity that would surely only help us. The deal I had done to create jobs, homes, a college and a shopping centre didn't matter. One thing politicians in marginal seats need to learn is that whatever your unique local achievements for your local community, they will only ever make so much difference when it comes to an election. The story today would be about John Prescott, who had decided to come and not return home. The footage was good on the six o'clock news. Politics these days is a strange blend between the important work of improving people's lives, which was something I was very good at, and being sprayed by the saliva of a high-profile politician in a short segment for the six o'clock news, which I was a bit less good at.

As for John Prescott, I don't see him just as a campaigner, more a force of nature.

CHAPTER 31

2005 – WINNING IN MY OWN RIGHT

T HE SECOND ELECTION you fight is more personal. It's an opportunity not just to judge your party, but to judge yourself and your work. Due to our majority being halved in 2001, Gloucester was one of the top thirty Tory target seats at the 2005 general election.

On the plus side, Iain Duncan Smith was the Tory leader and had not got to grips with his party since his appointment in 2001. My office in those days was in the Norman Shaw Buildings and I was a couple of doors along from a former Tory minister. He was in his wilderness days after the front bench and, I suspected, was among the many that had little time for their leader. When we were in the lift one day in the autumn of 2003 I pointed out the obvious: his boss had been mauled at PMQs again. I actually felt sorry for IDS. He muttered back something like, 'That'll be taken care of by Christmas.' I assumed he'd been on the red wine and I thought nothing more of it. Silly me, I should have been down the bookmakers.

Such is the brutality or hard-headedness (depending on your standpoint) of the Parliamentary Conservative Party that IDS was incinerated in a few short weeks of that conversation in the lift and replaced by Michael Howard in November 2003. Michael Howard was a very different proposition. He was never going to be loved by the public, but he was effective in the House of Commons chamber, which boosted Tory morale, and he knew how to organise. Although he deservedly had a hard-man reputation, after leaving the front bench a few years later he showed his softer side in a debate commemorating Holocaust Memorial Day. He talked about his Jewish roots and the tyranny of the Nazis. When I summed up the debate in the chamber, as the Minister for Faith Communities, I congratulated him on his input. I said that it was a very moving contribution, but that it wasn't the first time I'd found his speeches moving. He laughed as I told the House that some of his speeches had moved me enough to make me get off my backside and get into politics.

With Labour defending a 160-seat majority in 2005 it seemed inevitable that seats would be lost. Even though I had voted against it, the Iraq War was casting a long shadow and there was constant talk in the media of TB/GBs as Gordon's people pressed his claim for the top job. It led to some nervousness and instability in the Labour ranks in the run-up to 2005.

On the plus side for me, I had gone from being the Trot of Stoke Rochford Hall to being the model of good practice as a Labour MP in a marginal seat. The Labour press office was constantly in touch, wanting to put my name to quotes or putting me up for media opportunities. They knew I would do it well and I would get the line across, unruffled. The work I had done in the constituency was often showcased within the party as a model of best practice and my brilliant team of staff had helped put various presentations and packs together to show other MPs who needed a hand how we were campaigning in Gloucester.

Our record of achievement and investment for the constituency was, I truly believe, the very best in the country. Critics might say that it's typical for parties to flood marginal seats with cash. But I would have to say that if you don't fight for every penny then you don't get it – and just look at how poorly invested-in the place had been for so long.

The 2005 general election campaign was going pretty smoothly. The only difficulties tended to arise when Cabinet ministers arrived, which happened frequently.

One of the most comical moments was the arrival of a gold-coloured Jag. For some reason I still don't understand to this day, the party's organiser Paul Nicholson had been given this vehicle to drive around for a few days. Tessa Jowell the Culture Minister was visiting the constituency and, because we'd been so inundated with ministers, we didn't do anything elaborate – we just went out door-knocking in Barton. She was a London MP and we felt she'd

like it there: it's very multicultural and has rows of terraced housing. It has its rough parts, but so does every urban area.

It was a warm, sunny day and our activists were out in numbers.
The canvassing team that day had about twenty-five people in it
and off we went. David, Tricia and Rupi were 'running boards' – or
giving out the names and addresses and taking data from canvassers that would be fed into computers later in the day.

Paul the organiser drove around Barton in the gold Jag. He looked
like a drug dealer. Nonetheless, such was the enthusiasm of our door-
knockers and the Cabinet minister that we were hurtling through
the knock-up sheets, with posters going up, people coming out to
see what the excitement was all about and a gold Jaguar conspicu-
ously tailing us. Soon the canvassing sheets ran out. But everyone
wanted to keep going so we decided not to waste the opportunity
and continued knocking on doors and shaking hands blindly, without the data head office was always so focused on getting recorded.

The Jaguar somehow got separated from the group (I don't know
how – you couldn't miss it) so, for the next half an hour, Paul –
a nice well-spoken chap from the south coast – was left sweating
buckets, lost in Barton and being stared at by passers-by. And looking like a drug dealer. He was not happy.

I turned to Stuart Hudson, one of my team, and mentioned how
well it all seemed to be going, enquiring if Tessa was enjoying it.

'I left Tessa over there.'

'You what? What have you done with the Secretary of State, Stuart?'

'She went into a man's house, I think. She said she needed the
toilet.'

'You let her go? She's in some bloke's house on her own?'

'Well, Paul keeps ringing me. He's lost in the gold Jag and a bit miffed because we went the wrong way.'

A combination of lost gold Jaguars and lost ministers somewhere in Barton was not a good sign. Paul was angrily ringing people to find out what had gone wrong with his detailed canvassing plan but nobody was answering because people were either surging around the streets on the canvassing equivalent of a 'high' or stressing over lost members of the government. Thankfully, Tessa Jowell emerged from a terraced house before long. A charming West Indian gentleman came out and said: 'Anybody else need the toilet? Anything for the Labour Party.'

Tessa did an impromptu kerbside speech for the party members and was then driven away by one of her team to her next visit of the day. We finally found Paul back at the party office. The gold Jag was intact. It had been a good day and the fact he was cross because it hadn't been perfect was quite reassuring. I knew we were winning.

Only an earthquake could stop us.

Two days before polling day I had a proposition to consider. Paul said, 'We've been offered a leader's visit just before polling day. Do you want to take them up on it?'

It was a good question. These things are always tricky judgement calls. Not everyone takes up the offer – it can depend on a number of factors. But for me there was only ever one factor. My job as the candidate and as an experienced MP was to make a cold, hard judgement call on whether we were more likely or less likely to win with a visit. Nothing else – just winning in this particular seat and taking into account how the leader is perceived in the feedback from the doorstep and telephone data. There were no two ways about it:

the Iraq War was very unpopular locally and high-profile visits can go badly wrong as they are live televised events. (Think of Tony Blair being challenged outside a hospital in Birmingham in 2001; think of Gordon Brown, Mrs Duffy and the 'bigot' incident in Rochdale in 2010.) And if things are going well locally, do you want to risk it? If you turn it down you also need to hope that people accept it's a pragmatic decision purely based on securing another seat for the party in Parliament and not a personal slight on the leader or their entourage.

In 2010 I made those cold, hard judgements and decided a Gordon Brown visit a few days before polling day would not improve our chances. He wasn't going down well in Middle England areas like Gloucester from the data, and I knew it was likely to be close. By the same token, I had asked him to visit in 2007 during the floods because I thought it would help us politically and, more importantly, help us tackle the problems we were facing. And he had returned to make a second visit that week, which was also very welcome.

These are tough decisions at election time and emotion has to be put aside. It's all about winning, nothing else. My calculation in 2005, despite the war, was this: Gloucester was an unusual constituency; the number of middle-class and aspiring voters was unusually high for a Labour marginal and Blair's link to those voters, from our canvassing returns, still outweighed any detriment from the war, which was partly assuaged by my own opposition to it.

'Yes, we want him to come.'

Paul then told me they wanted to do a double bill: Gordon wanted to come too.

'Even better. He's the best Chancellor we've ever had and people like him. Let's do it.'

On Monday 1 May 2005, a phalanx of very assertive and bossy sharp-suited officials turned up and haggled with Paul, David from my office and Sheila Murphy from the regional office about what the visit the following day would look like. Goodness me, it was a shambles! The sharp suits could not settle on anything. Paul, David and Sheila offered them an assortment of treats to choose from – the new hospital, the new university campus, the new police headquarters, the new leisure centre and a number of new Sure Start centres were all suggested. During the course of the day they were all accepted, turned down, accepted again and then some other request would be made, like a local resident who had bought a home, a group of mums at a play centre or perhaps a golden goose laying eggs. I went to bed and left them to it. I could see our local people going barmy trying to get the suits to settle on a fixed idea. Ideally, one that wouldn't descend into farce when the PM and Chancellor came to town.

Come Tuesday morning, I was told what we were doing. They had set up some sort of wheel of fortune about house prices to get across the pitfalls of increased mortgage interest rates if the Tories should return to power. The theme was a 'home owner's economy'. They wanted about a hundred supporters to be present at the Trust Centre on Conduit Street. Had nobody told them that Conduit Street was next to the two mosques where opposition was greatest to the war? Whatever. I caballed a few thoughts about what I was going to say to introduce Gordon. Tony was still a well-kept secret. When we got to the Trust Centre I looked around the conference room. It was packed. All the big broadcasters were there. So was my family, lots of party members and friends. But, because of the constant last-minute chopping and changing of plans, I saw that there were also lots of people in that room who should not have been there – known troublemakers, loudmouths and some easily agitated protestors. The haphazard nature of the run-up meant there hadn't been any proper security checks or vetting of who was allowed in and who wasn't. I hoped for the best. The wheel of fortune was there, though, in the middle of the stepped stage.

I went downstairs to meet Tony, Gordon and Alastair Campbell, who were in a room next to the Sure Start centre. They were chipper. Alastair asked me how it was going and I said I thought we could increase our majority locally. 'Ah, typical local candidate! Thinks he can pull off a bigger majority, that's what we like to hear!' It was all very light and jokey. And for about the fiftieth time in twelve hours Alastair Campbell completely changed the plan for what was about to happen. The wheel of fortune was now redundant; I was to talk about the importance of the economy to the people of Gloucester, then introduce the two guests. They would join me on stage and each of them would talk about the economy. Then we'd come downstairs for photos with mums and babies in the Sure Start centre. There was no point in disagreeing or protesting, but it was a useful insight into how off-the-cuff things were at the heart of the election campaign.

So off I went upstairs, ready to make it up as we went along. I spoke for a few minutes about all the wonderful things we'd been able to achieve in Gloucester thanks to a growing economy. I then welcomed 'Gordon Brown Chancellor of the Exchequer and Labour Prime Minister Tony Blair'. The U2 track 'Beautiful Day' kicked in, much to my surprise. The people in the room thought I'd finally lost the plot because only Gordon was going to be there. And then they both strolled on to join me on the little stage. Gordon spoke for about ten minutes to a national audience about the need to not take risks with the economy. Tony then talked about where we were, tapped his feet and talked about the Sure Start centre below us. 'It's not that the Tories would oppose Sure Start, they just wouldn't ever have thought of it,' he said, before finishing with some rather embarrassing and gushing things about me and what I'd achieved. But that's why they were there in the first place.

The problem was, because the plans had chopped and changed, it just wasn't clear what was to happen after the applause had died down. The suits had said that interviews would happen downstairs, but nobody seemed to have told Tony and Gordon. After a slightly awkward moment when I was keen to get them the hell out while the going was good – and before someone made our lives really difficult on live TV – Tony gravitated towards Andrew Marr and started taking questions. With a room full of unvetted people, the inevitable happened: 'What about Iraq, Mr Blair?'

Oh no, I thought. He couldn't exactly walk away from this and I recognised the guy in overalls who was challenging the PM. He could do angry very well and he wouldn't have featured on the party's guest list for this event, for sure.

Tony edged towards him. I felt obliged to stay close to him. This was my patch and, however much I was fuming with the suits at that moment, we were in this together.

'What about Iraq?'

Every single microphone and TV camera was now within 3 feet of us. Thankfully some things are better out than in. Here is a snippet of how the BBC covered it:

CAMPAIGNING IN GLOUCESTER, MR BLAIR WAS CHALLENGED ABOUT HIS TRUSTWORTHINESS BY A MUSLIM VOTER, MOHAMMED JAFFER.

Mr Jaffer said: 'I think you have done a fantastic job of running this country, but foreign policy you need to look at really close up. We have lost hundreds of lives, thousands of lives. We got the impression you were just following President Bush.'

He later told reporters he would vote for Mr Blair if he just apologised to the British public and said 'Forgive me'. Mr Blair told Mr Jaffer prime ministers had to take difficult decisions and said it was the economy, the health service, schools and law and order which affected people.

In many respects, the party benefited from the fact that Tony had to face the voter and have the conversation – regardless of my blood pressure at the time. I should have been more relaxed about it. But, looking back, I can also understand my own anxiety.

Then, after an hour of bouncing babies on our knees downstairs in Sure Start and some similarly less taxing moments, it was time for them to leave. Getting out of the building and seeing them off was an experience because, by now, the whole world knew where they were. Protesters and supporters were packing the street, along with a significant uniformed presence. I wished them both luck at the next port of call, which was The Wrekin – a seat where we had an excellent MP in Peter Bradley, but unfortunately one we would not hold. We lost many good people that week.

. . .

Labour won the general election two days later, albeit with a majority of sixty-six compared to 160 in 2001. I was returned with an increase in my majority from 3,880 to 4,271 – one of the few seats to experience a swing to Labour.

Campaigning with Tony in 2005   *My re-election in 2005*

From a personal perspective it proved that some people in Gloucester who may have shied away from voting Labour in 2001 due to my race had been won round. My experience on the doorstep bore witness to that. People were frank with me when they said that they were wary of me because of what they had read in the paper. Some even confessed to ingrained racial prejudices, but said that having me as their MP for four years had changed their view.

I hope there is a lesson in that somewhere for political parties. They need to be braver. If they want to change the way society thinks for the better then they need to move obstacles that are blocking ordinary people from different racial backgrounds from being selected.

My re-election in 2005 was followed by my call-up to the Treasury benches as a member of Her Majesty's government, so my responsibilities became national and not just local. Taking a promotion when you hold a marginal seat is a risky business but turning it down would have been like a footballer turning down the chance to play for his country. And I wanted to do my bit to try to change my country.

.   .   .

This chapter is called 'Winning in my own right', but winning involved so many other people in my life. During my first term as an MP, a lot of special things happened to me – none more so than a fleeting encounter with someone in 2002 whom I would one day persuade to be my wife. She didn't know what I did for a living when we first set eyes on each other and despite all the things you learn about me in this book, she wasn't put off. Well, not too much, anyway.

We tied the knot in July 2003 in her hometown of Southampton. There would be some tough times ahead, not least the passing of her father just a few months after the 2005 election campaign. It was tough, but Rupi has an inner strength that got her through an intense election campaign despite the fact her father went under the knife on the day of the election. Sadly he passed away just a few months later, but not before we could give him some important news: Zac was already on his way.

Max would follow in March 2009 and the three of them would help me put the tough times into context and turn the good days into great days. And without Rupi's love and encouragement, this book would never have been written.

CHAPTER 32

THE WHIPS' OFFICE

THE INTENSITY OF the phone messages from the Blair and Brown camps congratulating me on my re-election in 2005 should have given me some indication of what was going on. But I was not schooled in the conventional political prep schools, so I just naively thought everyone was genuinely thrilled to have me back rather than competing for my affections as the TB/GBs ramped up around me. Rightly or wrongly, I was neither a Blairite nor a Brownite. I wasn't expecting a promotion after the 2005 election – not after my rebellion – but at the back of my mind I knew it could happen. I was good at my job.

I suspect my fate was kind of sealed when I drove in through the carriage gates on my first day back in the Commons. The little red sports car had been replaced by a black one – a Hyundai Coupe (which does actually have rear seats, but only for very small people). You have to wind your window down to show security your pass when you arrive at Parliament's carriage gates and, no sooner had I done so, a giant woolly microphone and a TV camera from *Channel 4 News* were thrust in my face. Before I knew what was going on, Gary Gibbon was throwing questions at me. 'That was a pretty bad election result for you guys, wasn't it? Is it time for your leader to go?'

I couldn't put my foot on the gas and drive off or it would look like I was ducking the question. So I just said what I thought: 'If you had told us before 1 May 1997 that Labour would be here in 2005, re-elected for a third term with a majority of over sixty, we'd have bitten your hands off for that.'

'And what about Tony Blair?'

'Great leader, great Prime Minister. Excuse me, I've got to get to work.'

And I put my foot down and went. It made for a good piece on the news. So, what do you do with good young communicators? You silence them. Within a couple of hours, Hilary Armstrong (Tony's Chief Whip) was on the phone telling me I'd been promoted to the Whips' Office. I had probably pleased the TBs and annoyed the GBs without even thinking about it as I drove into work.

I never wanted to be a whip. You're not allowed to speak in the chamber any more, your constituents don't hear your voice on the Parliament Channel or on the Andrew Neil show and you can't even sign early day motions. Goodbye media and hello to the world of thumb screws and arm-twisting. Hilary reassured me it would be a great stepping-stone to the despatch box and I'd be a much better minister for understanding the intricacies of Westminster – an education I would only receive with a spell as a whip. I decided I'd give it a year and if that didn't work out I could always go back to the backbenches.

A part of me wondered if this was a funny kind of punishment for voting against the war. The irony wasn't lost on my colleagues that I was now a whip and the only member of the government who hadn't voted to invade Iraq. I asked for permission to whip for the DTI department. Alan Johnson was the Secretary of State there and was a good guy to work with. The department had just changed its name from DTI to Productivity, Energy, Industry and Science, with the unfortunate acronym of PEnIS – so it was soon changed back to DTI. It was easier to say you were the DTI whip.

I was not a natural whip. I couldn't bully or threaten; I could only cajole and reason. As the government pushed controversial reforms like foundation hospitals, academy schools, longer detention for terror suspects and a renewal of Trident, the PLP got harder to manage. I got on with it, grafted and kept my head down, focusing on my truculent MPs and getting my DTI legislation through the House. On one occasion Labour lost a vote in the Commons by one when the Prime Minister had been allowed to leave early. On another occasion we won a vote by one when I saw an MP from the 2005 intake walking into the wrong lobby (I won't name him but he knows who he is). He was trying to sneak into the 'no lobby'. When I caught him I politely told him that the government were voting 'aye'. He thanked me and turned around but, from the look in his eye, I think we both knew exactly what he was up to.

By the time a year had gone by, I was ready to call it a day. I'd just about got the hang of it but I was getting Whips' Office cabin fever. Nobody could blame me for leaving government at the reshuffle: I had a new and kicking excuse to spend time with my family. Zachery Singh Dhanda had been born on New Year's Day 2006. We were in Gloucester, in our new family home on Painswick Road, watching the reshuffle unfold on Sky News. And then the phone rang.

CHAPTER 33

YES, MINISTER

I MISSED THE CALL initially. I must have popped to the loo. I don't know why I said 'I must have'– the fact of the matter is I had. Typical. You wait thirty-four years for the call and then discover you missed out on being promoted because of a call of nature. Rupi answered it and was visibly tingling with excitement. I was deadpan with her.

'I wouldn't get your hopes up...'

'I know, I know, I know! Just ring it. Now!'

So I did. I rang the No. 10 switchboard and said I thought the boss wanted to talk to me. I was put through to a lovely lady who knew me but, I must confess, with it just being a telephone I had no idea who she was. She was very excited for me though. By now my stomach was doing somersaults. Zac was lying on the sofa next to his mummy and seemed unusually quiet. I'd recited the little Sikh prayer in my head that my mother had taught me as a child, not to ask for a promotion but just to prepare me for whatever news was coming my way.

'I'm afraid he's on the phone to someone else, darling!' said the nice lady. 'Can he ring you back?'

Well, I couldn't really say no, could I? But my curiosity was getting the better of me. 'Is it … you know … is it good news?'

She had a very chirpy voice: 'If it's the same as Gilly I think so, yes.' She must've meant Gilly Merron, the MP for Lincoln, one of my friends from the Whips' Office.

Well, all I could do was sit down and wait. And hope he would ring me back. It was just a few minutes. It was one of the ladies from the No. 10 switchboard: 'We have the Prime Minister for you.'

You can't really prepare yourself for a conversation like that. I can't, anyway. I needed to know but I couldn't help but prattle on with small talk about how it was all going.

'Well, you know,' he said. And I kind of did. It was Friday 5 May 2006, the day after a bad set of local council elections for Labour nationally and the media were reporting that he'd been bounced into doing his reshuffle earlier than planned because some of Gordon's people were coming out in a co-ordinated way to call for a timetable for a handover. 'Parmjit, you've been doing a good job – would you like to be Parliamentary Undersecretary of State at the Department for Education?'

I couldn't believe my luck and was momentarily lost for words. Some weeks earlier Peter Hain, the Northern Ireland Secretary, had suggested to me that he'd really like to have me as a minister in his department if the opportunity came along. I'd got it into my head that if it was going to happen I'd be going there. No disrespect to Northern Ireland, but Education would have been top of my wish list as a boy from a state education in west London.

I managed to cough up the words 'Education – I'd be delighted, Tony' for Rupi's benefit, to keep her in the loop. As she thrust her arms in the air I told him that I was deeply grateful for the opportunity and that I wouldn't let him down or ever forget the faith he'd shown in me. And he had. The following day Cherie Blair called to congratulate me. They were obviously under some pressure from the neighbours and she was doing her bit to help her husband. But she needn't have worried. After my rebellion in 2003 many a Prime Minister would have just shut the door on me. Both Tony and Cherie showed an interest in my family, my constituency and me as a person. He even initiated a couple of conversations with me about Sikhism, he genuinely wanted to know more about it. That's not me being a sycophantic Blairite, and I'm well aware of how unfashionable it is to say nice things about Tony – I'm just speaking as I found from my personal experience. Right or wrong, I've been brought up to be good to people who are nice to me.

Just to remind you that I am an Indian boy, the first thing I did after the Prime Minister's call was to ring my parents. And to remind me that they are Indian parents, they cried. Over the next year I would visit and open many Sure Start centres as we met our promise to build 3,000 of them across the country. I was straight to work on Monday in the department, preparing to take the Children and Adoption Bill through its parliamentary stages the following day. Within days of that I was introducing a bill that enhanced safeguarding measures for children and vulnerable adults. I was also heavily involved in producing the Care Matters Green Paper, one of Alan Johnson's priorities as Secretary of State. We worked to improve the lives of the 30,000 children in the care system. One of the most satisfying roles any politician from any party could have.

· · ·

In July 2007 Gordon Brown became Prime Minister and I served in his government as Minister for the Fire and Rescue Service and Minister for Community Cohesion in the Department for Communities and Local Government (CLG). I had a wonderful range of responsibilities there from race and faith, to local government, planning and digital inclusion. I'm particularly proud to have been part of a major change programme at the fire and rescue service where we shifted the focus from fighting fires to saving more lives through fire prevention measures like the installation of hundreds of thousands of smoke detectors. I'm really grateful to the fire community and my former officials for overcoming some, shall we say initial concerns, to embrace my ideas to double the number of women recruited to the service and to reward fire authorities that recruited 5 per cent BAME firefighters above the local population. They helped change the service for the better.

CHAPTER 34

WHAT COULD
POSSIBLY GO WRONG?

I GOT ON WITH my job as the internal squabbling slowly spread in the Labour Party. It was sad and it was messy but I was determined to stay out of it and try to focus on being a good MP, a good minister and a good parent with Rupi. But an accumulation of problems was going to make life difficult. As an MP you've got to deal with problems. Here is a little selection of some of the things that kept me awake at night:

1. International terrorism in Gloucester

Yes, you did read that correctly. In 2003 the rise of radical Islamist activity in the UK impacted directly on Gloucester. This culminated in the arrest of Saajid Badat, a former local grammar school boy who lived with his family in the heart of Barton. His arrest caused a huge surge of anger among the local Muslim community, which the local police initially handled badly. Their local PR people thought it would be a good idea to hold a public meeting in a community centre in the week of the arrest, and then invite all and sundry to it, including the world's media. The media was then invited to film the spectacle of 200 angry people (some of whom were whipped up by people who knew better) yelling 'Free our boy, he's innocent' at the senior police officer who was put up on the stage and 'Sack Home Secretary David Blunkett' and 'Are you for us or against us?' at me, also standing on the podium. (I thought the meeting was a crazy idea but it would have been even worse if I hadn't taken up their invitation, albeit reluctantly.)

They saved the greatest venom for the local newspaper, whose deputy editor was also put up on the podium and who tried to justify having stuck the story on the front page with the guy's birth certificate. The deputy editor looked relieved to escape the meeting alive and told me he feared that his offices might get burnt down. And, thanks to the constabulary's PR team, this was all played out on BBC *Newsnight* cameras and *Today* programme microphones. To add to the venom, the Socialist Workers Party had people travelling in from Bristol, extremist group Al Majouroun (never ones to miss a recruiting opportunity) had bussed people down from

Birmingham, and a few white, middle-class lefties had jumped off the Stroud peace bus, which I believe had just come back from Baghdad, to shout out – to the acclaim of the crowd – 'We're here to show solidarity with oppressed brown-faced people!' Well, this particular brown-faced person wasn't impressed with people coming from afar to whip up what was already a sensitive situation.

My goodness, what a mess. I appealed for calm and reason. I said I would meet with and talk to David Blunkett (which I did) but they as a community had a responsibility to wait and see how the legal process panned out. There is good and bad in every community. I repeated that mantra for the *Today* programme too, but it was a very difficult time for Gloucester. The good, decent, silent majority was drowned out.

But when I visited Scotland Yard a few days later for a private briefing, I realised I had done exactly the right thing. Badat had a training shoe, a detonator and enough explosives in his house to blow a hole in an airliner. Small wonder he confessed in the back of the squad car as soon as they picked him up. That shut the hotheads up for a while.

Yet the impact of the Badat arrest alerted the authorities to something I had been becoming increasingly aware of myself: radicalisation was a growing problem and would take up more of my time.

2. The Southall by-election and Labour's diversity problem

Piara Khabra, the first Sikh MP, died at the age of eighty-six in June 2007, leaving us with the headache of a by-election. Within a week of Piara's death, Gordon Brown, Labour's newly anointed Prime Minister, was doing his first reshuffle. He rang me to ask if I would take a ministerial role in the Department for Communities and asked for my help in the Southall by-election. I agreed to do both, and moved back to my parents' home for a month to help run the campaign. I had a sense of duty to Southall and ran myself into the ground there in the coming weeks, whilst also trying to manage my new departmental responsibilities.

That month I saw at first hand how the disconnect between my party and ethnic minority voters was growing. Our attitude towards the community, from candidate selection to how we used local knowledge to campaign and engage on issues, was through the prism of 'this is a problem we have to deal with' rather than a sense of ownership and genuine engagement with a savvy and supportive community.

A survey in the *Daily Telegraph* in December 2014 suggests that my fears in the Southall by-election in 2007 were well placed:

LABOUR'S CRUCIAL ETHNIC MINORITY VOTE SET TO COLLAPSE

Influential pollsters say that Labour are mistaken in their belief they are 'sitting pretty' with the ethnic minority vote as Indian, Pakistani and African voters are turning away from the party in huge numbers.

The number of Indian voters identifying with the Labour Party has fallen from 77 per cent in 1997 to just 18 per cent in 2014 – a fall of over three-quarters, according to figures from the British Election Study.

Pakistani support has fallen from 77 to 57 per cent, a fall of 27 per cent. Meanwhile Caribbean support has dropped 14 per cent from 78 to 67 per cent.

Support from the African community has dropped by 20 per cent, from 79 to 63 per cent, the research shows.

Proud men and women of Indian and other ethnic heritages – who had served Southall through the riots, the anti-Nazi marches and the years of mass recruitment to gain control of their local Labour Party – felt brushed aside and were lining up to give it to me in the neck. They weren't happy that, as proud community representatives, their advice on how to run their own campaign was being ignored. They felt their relationship with the party chiefs was like a colonial relationship from the days of the Raj, not helped by the division of duties between two election centres, with the white people mostly based outside the constituency in Acton and the Asians grafting and isolated in a dilapidated centre above a shop on Southall Broadway. This was largely a perception problem, but perceptions matter. It fomented an attitude that they were voting fodder, often asked to line up behind Cabinet members (all white) who marched behind *dhol* drummers along Southall Broadway, literally drumming up support.

It was visible and effective campaigning, but it wasn't a replacement for engagement and for making people feel part of the Labour Party and its policies. There was an undercurrent of 'them and us' and I had constant complaints from local party members that they felt demeaned by it. As I said earlier, they felt like a problem to be dealt with rather than part of the solution.

As the link person between them and the party, it was my job to take this on the chin and to keep them focused on winning, which I did. I talked to colleagues about my concerns but a new regime was asserting itself in the Labour Party and my feedback wasn't welcome. I sensed that very strongly.

So I just dug in, bit my tongue and worked hard out all day on the streets, campaigning with the candidate and the local activists. They were not fools; they knew what they were talking about. However bad the process, we had a good candidate in Virendra Sharma – a friend of mine of many years' standing. We won by over 5,000 but I felt the result was papering over the cracks of a greater malaise that had to be put right or we would suffer in the long term.

Piara Khabra had massively upset the party establishment by deselecting the incumbent MP in 1992. He believed in taking control. Sikhs are cremated and never buried. Just as well, because he would have been turning in his grave at the thought of ceding such authority to outsiders.

My own research published in *The Guardian* in 2014 gave me greater cause for worry. It suggested that, in terms of ethnic minority representation, Parliament is going backwards in both the Commons and the Lords. Nationally BAME communities make up 14 per cent of our country, and that's growing fast. Yet only 4 per cent of the House of Commons – or twenty-seven MPs – are from ethnic minority backgrounds. If Parliament were proportionate to the electorate there would be over ninety. Ethnic minority voters represent 20 per cent of Labour MPs' constituents now, yet only 6 per cent of their MPs.

The reality is that my election in 2001 didn't open the floodgates for a more representative society, but it may have actually led to some complacency. People could point to me and say: 'There you are, look what we've achieved.' Likewise, people will see people like Keith Vaz or Diane Abbott on TV and assume there are dozens of Labour MPs like them, not realising that they were elected back in 1987. In 2010 the number has only expanded to sixteen out of 257 Labour MPs. Worryingly, whilst I've been calling for a step change in Labour's approach to diversity, the Tories have been catching up with us in their number of ethnic minority MPs.

My parents' generation look back to when they arrived in the 1960s and cannot believe the lack of progress in this area. I can't believe the extent to which I and others have failed to make a difference to these appalling stats and the survey results from the *Telegraph*.

My fear is that the barriers I have talked about in this book are still very much in place across all the political parties.

3. Floods and the loss of water supply

The day after the Southall by-election it rained all the way home to Gloucester. I was tired and desperate to get to my family home for some rest. But it kept raining and by the time I was back a large chunk of Longlevens in my constituency was underwater and many of the roads blocked. I headed straight to Longlevens to meet David from my office and staff from the Environment Agency to see how bad it was. In my suit I waded around in water up to my knees

– I hadn't had time to go home, let alone pick up some wellies! It wasn't good: dozens of homes were flooded out.

That night I went to the leisure centre, which had become a temporary home for 600 people who had been stranded due to flooding along the railway lines. I was back the following morning to check on how things were progressing and to ensure there were supplies for everyone. I learnt that, across the county, 2,000 people had spent the night in centres like this one. When it rains, it pours.

I spoke to Gordon Brown on the phone to brief him on what was happening. It turned out to be worse than I'd thought. Come Sunday I was asked to join a ministerial conference call chaired by the Floods Minister, my CLG colleague (not that I'd had much chance to spend time in my office) John Healey. Apparently Gloucestershire's Mythe water treatment works had become contaminated by flood water. The people of Gloucestershire could be without water in their taps for a fortnight. *A fortnight!* I couldn't believe it.

Although I'd hardly seen them for a month I thought it best to send Rupi and Zac to London so I didn't have to worry about them while I got on top of my latest major headache. I then headed to the county's Gold Command centre at the new police HQ in my constituency to get a proper handle on things. After a month in Southall I was destined to spend much of the next fortnight in Gold Command. That night I rang Gordon again. Poor soul sounded even more tired than me. But I needed to let him know this wasn't just about hundreds of flooded-out families any more. We were now due to lose water supply in large chunks of the county that very night and, as the rain kept falling, we were within millimetres of a power substation in Walham, on the outskirts of Gloucester, flooding. If we lost it, we would be without electricity as well as water. There was a danger we could be about to return to medieval times in the county, with no water or electricity for an undetermined period of time. In Gold Command we even talked about mass-scale evacuation in the event of hospitals being unable to maintain power. The threat of large-scale civil disobedience was also in our minds in the event of us all being plunged into darkness. The army was very much a part of the planning for difficult scenarios.

We made arrangements for Gordon to be helicoptered into Gloucester at 7.30 a.m. It would be good for him, good for me and, most importantly, reassuring for the British public to see him on the scene of the crisis.

Fighting the floods with Gordon Brown

The visit went well, although it was just at the command centre. The army and the fire-fighters managed to stop the power substation from flooding, which reportedly could have blacked out the county and much of south Wales. But the crisis was then about the loss of water supply, which wasn't restored properly until 2 August.

Local people were remarkably stoic and looked out for each other in a way I'll never forget, taking water supplies to each other's homes and waiting patiently at bowsers. After PMQs on Wednesday that week – less than a week after the by-election – Gordon, Laurence Robertson (the Tory MP for Tewkesbury) and some of Gordon's team helicoptered back into Gloucester together to view the distribution of water in the city (we were still without water), thank those who had been involved in saving the substation (at least we had electricity) and meet people who had been affected in both Gloucester and Tewkesbury. We did well to survive the crisis. But, for my office, it would be the tip of the iceberg, as we would have many months of follow-up with the many families who had lost their homes. The recovery work had only just begun.

• • •

So, other than international terrorism, the establishment's disengagement with minority communities, floods and loss of water supplies, everything was hunky-dory!

CHAPTER 35

MEETING THATCHER

I T WAS REMEMBRANCE Sunday 2007. In many ways it was
very different to any Remembrance Sunday I'd experienced
before. For starters, in all the years I was an MP this would be
the one and only year that I would not be laying a wreath at the
Gloucester war memorial.

I was Her Majesty's Minister for the Fire and Rescue Service, and
therefore my duties included attending the national war memorial
in London, where I would lay a wreath on behalf of the fire service.

It would be a day to live long in my memory for many reasons
– not least for the first, last and only conversation I would have

with Margaret Thatcher. It was a very bizarre conversation indeed, which I will come to in a moment. But the whole day was a bit surreal, to be honest.

The idea of being in the same room as Thatcher went against the grain of my entire upbringing in the first place, let alone the thought of entering into a conversation with her. In fairness to her, if she had not existed I'd never have become politicised in the first place. The only previous occasion I was in her proximity was after the Queen Mother's death in April 2002. The Queen Mother was brought to lie in state in Westminster Hall in Parliament and I had decided to attend the ceremony to mark the arrival of the coffin. All MPs were invited.

The decision to attend was tinged slightly with misplaced guilt. Misplaced because I wasn't responsible for the Queen Mother's death and misplaced because there was nothing wrong with me having spent the long bank holiday weekend beforehand on a lads' break in Tenerife having fun. But being young and single was never a good enough excuse to be able to relax and do the normal things in life my friends could do – not in my mind, anyway. I was ridiculously self-conscious about enjoying myself while having such a serious job. Hence the guilt.

When I got back from holiday I received letters from some constituents about the service in Westminster Hall and I thought, fair enough, if that's what they want from their MP then I'll go. In any case, you couldn't criticise the Queen Mother's service in the war years, so I'd at least show up and arrange for a few of my dyed-in-the-wool Tory constituents to come along and pay their respects too. The fact that those dyed-in-the-wool constituents became good friends after my office sorted out the trip for them was not a bad thing either.

There weren't many MPs at the service. They were obviously still out on the tiles in the Canaries or whatever they were doing over Easter, so I was shuffled into a more prominent position than a relatively new backbencher would have expected or deserved, alongside the great and the good in the front row – mostly military types from assorted nations around the globe. I'd never even met the Queen Mother and I felt such a fraud!

As I left the service, I was directly behind Tony and Cherie Blair. And then it happened. Baroness Margaret Thatcher gingerly got up from her seat and stepped in front of me: the woman I had despised in my youth; the woman I would have bludgeoned as a teenager to save the country from a generation of unemployment, cuts, division and misery. She walked slowly in front of me, just behind Tony and Cherie. I could have reached down and lifted her hat off her head. Or done far worse damage to her had I still despised her so. But the truth, as I realised in that moment (if there was ever any doubt in my mind), was that, for all she represented to me in the 1980s, my youthful political anger had dissipated when faced with the real world.

And, in any case, it was 2002. Yes, she was this historical figure it was still fashionable on the left to hate, but, at the end of the day, she was getting frail and was physically a smaller human being than the Maggie of her heyday. The fact that my boss, the first Labour Prime Minister in nearly twenty years, was just two paces in front of us may have crossed my mind for a millisecond or two as well.

So that was April 2002, the last I thought I'd ever see of Maggie within judo range. Until Remembrance Sunday 2007.

I was now a minister and, much to the humour of my wife, somebody who had to begin the morning in the square of the Foreign Office court inspecting the guard. There was an assortment of emergency services and shiny-buttoned military standing to order and I had to inspect them. I walked up and down the aisles, my back as straight as could be, giving an occasional regal nod and pausing to give the occasional word or two of encouragement as they stood saluting and stuff like that. At least I think that's what I was supposed to do. I must have missed the day we were taught 'inspecting the military guard' at Mellow Lane Comp.

I looked up to the balcony in this historic-looking courtyard where Rupi, replete in her new hat, was standing with, from recollection, Sir Ronnie Flanagan, head of the RUC and Mrs Jack Straw. I couldn't look at her for too long for fear she'd wet herself laughing. I felt a right berk but I kept going.

I stayed sombre, saw it through and think I did it well. But if you come from where I come from, you spend half your time trying to hide the awe you feel for the people doing the saluting when you're meant to come across with a commanding air. That's why public school kids, especially the Old Etonians, have one over on the likes of me in Parliament: most of them have been trained to think this is somehow normal behaviour.

When I'd finished doing the official stuff I went up to the balcony and whispered: 'I didn't eff that up, did I?'

She gave me a discreet pat on the bottom and said: 'Have you done that before?' I took that as tacit approval.

Wreaths were laid by prime ministers past and present as we observed from the Foreign Office balcony overlooking the war memorial. Then a silence was impeccably observed. As the newest member of the establishment, I was almost done for the day.

But if I was part of the establishment I was soon to be reminded that I shouldn't be so sure of myself in such exultant company.

The Locarno Suite is a very plush room in the Foreign Office. It's the room the great and the good retire to after the wreaths have been laid on Remembrance Sunday. Baroness Cathy Ashton, at that time Labour's leader of the House of Lords, came over to Rupi and me to check we were OK and all had gone well. As we were talking, Rupi pointed out Baroness Thatcher at the other end of the room. 'Look, it's Maggie,' she said. Before I could shush her Cathy asked us if we'd like to be introduced.

'Nope,' I said.

But then the two of them ganged up on me. 'Oh, go on! Get over yourself! What harm can it do?' Truth be told, I was a little curious, and I was confident that I wouldn't do anything silly. The Duke of Edinburgh incident was years ago. Plus I hadn't laid a glove on her in 2002 at the Queen Mother's service.

So there we were, slaloming between the dignitaries with Baroness Ashton, off to meet the Iron Lady. Then Cathy whispered in her ear as Rupi and I stood alongside her. Cathy let her know there was someone she'd like her to meet.

Mrs Thatcher looked at me; I didn't turn to stone. I wasn't even scared. She looked ever so slightly bemused by me. I leaned down to talk to her.

'Hello, Baroness Thatcher.' I said it slowly and clearly and she looked back at me. It wasn't much of a chat-up line but I followed up with my name and the fact I was the Member of Parliament for Gloucester, which I knew was a bit of a spin-out for many a Tory younger than Mrs T.

To put her at her ease, I said: 'Sally Oppenheim. Sally was the MP for Gloucester when you were Prime Minister. She was one of your ministers, Mrs Thatcher.'

At that point I thought we'd connected. She looked around the room for a moment, no doubt recalling Oppenheim and the many ministers junior and senior she'd held in her charge in the Downing Street days. And here I was. Like one of the establishment, in the Locarno Suite, talking to the most famous Prime Minister of my lifetime.

Her eyes returned to me and she spoke.

'Which country are you from?' she said.

CHAPTER 36

TAKING ON COMRADE
BOB CROW

THERE I WAS in Eland House in Bressenden Place, Victoria. These were not the ivory towers of Whitehall. This was the home of CLG. The Department for Communities and Local Government.

However much Eland House had the décor of my old school huts, I was loving the job as a minister in this department between 2007 and 2008. The mix of responsibilities had me covering: the fire and rescue service; community cohesion (including being Minister for

Race and Faith); bits of local government; the Audit Commission; and planning in London, the East Midlands and the south-east. I even had e-governance in my bailiwick. Welcome to the world of politics and the hotch-potch of responsibilities you are given.

But it was a really good job with decent officials who didn't block radical changes I made to policies in the fire service to reform it, setting new targets for ethnic minority recruitment, shifting the focus from fire-fighting to fire prevention and installing a modernisation project with new kit, trucks, engines and fire stations. Talk about boys with their toys.

Then, one day, word got about that the RMT union was in town. I could feel the ripples of fear on the seventh floor of Eland House as officials strived to get on top of every aspect of their briefs. I was joshing with my private secretary Ian about which poor unsuspecting minister was about to get their comeuppance from Comrade Bob Crow's boys.

'Actually, it's not just Bob's boys,' said Ian. 'Bob's going to part of the delegation.'

Aha, no wonder they were all so worried. Bob's reputation as being a ball-buster of a trade union general secretary was something he was very proud of. He was a rare breed – a combination of historic trade union artefact and basher of New Labour, but adored by the old left and his membership.

I laughed: 'So which poor sucker's going to get the hairdryer treatment?!'

Ian smiled. 'Minister, the RMT want to talk about health and safety on the London Underground. That's one for you, Fire Minister.'

My heart sank.

Come the morning of the meeting I was quite chilled out. I'd never met Bob before, but I had pretty good working-class and trade union credentials. And, after all, how bad could he be? Well, the level of activity among the civil service told me something. The briefing notes kept pouring in. Yet more 'lines to take' crossed my desk. The morning banter and the smiling faces were replaced by taciturn expressions. By the time we'd decamped to the large meeting room I was worried that my officials would be hurling themselves out of the seventh-floor windows before the RMT arrived.

By this time I'd had enough. As the massed ranks of the RMT arrived (I think there were half a dozen in all) I decided to just head for the door, be informal and greet them all with warm handshakes. I invited them all to sit around the table for a cup of tea and a biscuit – it's what my mum would have done.

Bob was one of the first to come in. I was surprised – he wasn't 7 ft tall after all. And he wasn't breathing fire out of his nostrils. Maybe he was lulling me into a false sense of security.

I sat down in my seat at the head of the table – minister in Her Majesty's government and upright to chair this meeting – using every inch of my considerable height.

Bob had taken a seat right at the very end of the table, furthest from me and on the right. It had to be a cunning old trade union ploy.

I cleared my throat to start the meeting. 'Welcome, everybody. Before we do introductions and get to business, I just want you to know I have no fixed agenda here. Neither does my department.

I want to work with you on safety issues and I know my officials will agree with me on that.'

There was a slight murmur of approval.

As the conversation rolled for the next forty-five minutes, barely ten seconds could go by without my beady eyes turning to Bob at the end of the table, slightly hidden by a burly RMT colleague. As the clock ticked by the RMT officials made their points about what could be looked at and the regulations that should be considered. I agreed, backed up by my officials, that we would work hand in glove on these matters. And then it was over. Bob hadn't spoken.

I felt my shoulders relax and shook the comrades' hands as they left the room. *Do come again*, I thought, *but not until my officials have restocked their sedatives.* Then there was just one left. Comrade Bob. I shook his hand and he held me in his vice-like grip. *Please don't head-butt me*, I thought as he leaned in.

'Oi, minister,' he whispered in a Bob Hoskins-like manner. 'Minister, your driver.'

My driver? I was perplexed. 'You mean Steve Doyle, my ministerial driver?'

'Yeah, Steve Doyle.'

What on earth had he done? All I could think to say was, 'Yes, Steve. He's a … he's a … good guy.'

Bob edged a little closer. 'Millwall fan,' he said. 'Millwall fan like me.'

Aha! I relaxed and firmed up my grip. Of course, you could tell from my driver's many tattoos that he was a Millwall fan, and a serious one too. But I can forgive people most things in life and

Steve was a really decent bloke. And you can bet that having him around and on your side made you feel pretty safe too.

'Of course, Bob – you're both Millwall fans!'

Bob smiled. Stepped back. Looked serious for a moment and said: 'Give him an effing pay rise.' Then he left.

Rest in peace, Comrade.

END OF THE STORY

CHAPTER 37

END OF THE PARTY

OLLEAGUES WERE WHISPERING in my ears that I was set for another promotion to the rung just below Cabinet, but the tingling of blades in my back told me that I'd be levered out of government. The fact that I wasn't a signatory of the letter in 2006 calling for Tony Blair to go so we could get on with an orderly transition to Gordon didn't bode well for me either.

The phone rang. 'Punjit. Punjit, it's Gordon Brown.'

Of course it was. Nobody else called me 'Punjit'.

I thought to myself: 'Gordon, you might as well save yourself the breath. I've already been phoned by a journalist who has been briefed by your team that you're giving my job to Sadiq Khan.' We went through a bizarre charade for a few minutes where he couldn't come to terms with the fact he was sacking me. In fact, he even told me he was 'promoting' me.

'Gordon, just say it as it is, please.'

But no, he wanted to promote me 'in my constituency'. Ah, that kind of promotion. Unfortunately, government was becoming so dysfunctional and divided by 2008 that all manner of posts were being created to appease those who were being 'promoted' as a means of softening their sacking. People were being made 'party vice-chairs' for sunny parts of the globe or 'envoys' to whatever their personal hobby horse was. I had the opportunity to create one too but I politely declined.

Although he had in mind for me the chair role of a regional committee in the south-west of England (a role that hadn't been created yet and frankly was not in the gift of a Prime Minister), I would have been much happier if he had just said: 'Thanks, mate, but time's up and I want to clear space for someone else.'

That's politics and that's life. I'm sure he was trying to be kind by telling me the regional chairs would be paid posts, but it got my back up. Perhaps I'm stupid, but I have this rather irrational pride thing. It's inherited and goes with the working-class Punjabi thing. I declined and said I'd much rather just be on the backbenches.

Zac was approaching the age of three and had only known life crawling over red boxes to play with Daddy. And Rupi was pregnant with Max. The Labour Party was in a painful descent that was destined to result in defeat in 2010. It wasn't a bad time for me to find some joy in politics again. Do something daft, perhaps even run for Speaker of the House one day...

CHAPTER 38

REVIVAL – RUNNING FOR SPEAKER

L ABOUR HAD REACHED it pre-election nadir. On Thursday 4 June 2009 the party was battered in the local elections and came third in the European parliamentary elections, level with UKIP on seats and behind them in terms of votes. James Purnell, Hazel Blears and Caroline Flint had resigned and the party was fracturing badly.

This was the first time in British electoral history that a party in government had been outpolled in a national election by a party with no representation in the House of Commons. But, worst of all, the BNP won two seats – its first ever success in a nationwide election.

I locked myself away in Gloucester, depressed and frustrated about the state of my party, its inability to respond to the expenses scandal, its constant lurching from crisis to crisis and its inability to communicate with ordinary people, let alone Middle England.

One night, I'd just slumped on the sofa at home after putting Zac to bed. Rupi came in with baby Max asleep in her arms, who was then three months old. The news was on the TV and it didn't brighten my mood.

'Look,' said Rupi, 'Michael Martin has just resigned as Speaker over the expenses crisis.' I could see that. It had been bound to happen anyway.

Then she said something quite odd and interesting for some-one who claims not to be that interested in politics: 'Babe, you should run for it.'

'Are you mad? I'd have no chance. In any case, John Bercow already has it sewn up. He's been campaigning for the job for over a year.'

'Darling, who said anything about winning? You don't have to win the contest to win the arguments, do you? I've had to lis-ten to you moaning about everything that's wrong – well, you've got good ideas. You might never get another chance to show how things should be done again. Stuff Parliament. After those two idi-ots from the BNP just got elected maybe the country will sit up and listen to something sensible a fresh face has to say. Don't tell me everyone's become a racist overnight; they just can't stand any of you lot at the moment. Sorry, honey – but your lot are as crap as the others at the moment!'

Before I could take exception to that, she'd left the room with Max and I was alone to ponder.

In the next twelve days, my love for politics was reignited. I put my head together with quality young political minds to work up an offer that would appeal not to the House but to the country. We wanted to be bold and radical. James Green from my West-minster office showed me some work that Steve Richards of *The Independent* had done that resonated with where we were coming from. As the other nine candidates – all good establishment fig-ures with knighthoods and seals of office from the Privy Council – talked about their CVs, MP salaries and the status of 'the House', we talked about the need for a new and more deferential politics, with debates leaving the capital, the chucking-out of established parliamentary protocols to make democracy more direct, and the use of new technology to let the public have a say on our agenda. And the creation of a Parliament that looked more like the society it no longer represented.

I soon had the fifteen nominations from MPs I needed to make the hustings on 22 June in the packed chamber. But, before then, because what I was saying was so counterposed to the other nine narratives, we started making waves nationally. Sam Coates of *The Times*, John Craig of Sky, Shaun Ley of the BBC and Nick Lestor from the lobby were among those who gave lift-off in the media to what was becoming a radical campaign. On the road to the 22nd there were several debates with the candidates and, courtesy of the *FT*, PoliticalBetting.com and many journalists, I got written up as the winner. I never spoke from notes in the campaign; I just spoke from the heart, but with a clear narrative for change.

I felt alive again. Here is the speech I gave to the House that day. For the record, I finished seventh out of ten, beating a few knights of the realm along the way. But the speech did get the best write-ups and John Bercow tells me to this day that, if it were down to performance on the day, I would probably have won it. That was very kind of him, but I wasn't there to become Speaker. I wanted to paint a picture of how politics and our democracy should look rather than of the embattled and insular mess it was becoming.

> *Mr Parmjit Dhanda (Gloucester) (Lab)*: Nearly there; this is the last one.
>
> I have been in this race for twelve days. I have been play-ing catch-up because others have probably been in it for twelve months or perhaps longer – who knows? The key thing that brought me into this in the first place was a sense of frustration.
>
> I listened to all nine contributions. Actually, I passionately believe that any of the ten of us is capable of doing the job of Speaker. However, I ask myself and colleagues in the House: *Do we all really get it?* Do we understand the extent of crisis out there and the level of people's anger? I am not sure that we do.
>
> We have seen ourselves on the front pages of national and local newspapers day in, day out, and as the main item on news bulletins day in, day out. Then, two Sundays ago, we had the results of the European elections, which mean that two of our representatives in the European Parliament come

from the British National Party. That should send us a very strong message. The message is not that the British people are racists – I do not believe that they are – but they are telling us that they are thoroughly disengaged with us. They think that this place is remote and distant from them and that we are remote and distant from them as well.

So, what do we do now? That is the challenge and the question that we are being asked today. The easy and safe thing would be to retreat to someone who is a safe pair of hands – an establishment candidate. We have no end of quality candidates with great ideas, and we have heard from them today. We have half a dozen knights of the realm and Privy Counsellors – as I said the other day, there are probably more gongs than you will see at the Olympic Games – but are they in touch and do they speak the language of modern Britain? Part of the question that we need to ask ourselves is whether we will be thanked tomorrow for our choice.

My proposals are quite different from what all the other candidates are talking about. We need to change the settlement between the citizen and Parliament. We need a more deferential Parliament and to give more power away to local people and communities – that is the way to re-engage with local people.

In this day and age, when the rest of the public – our constituents – are using Facebook, Twitter and the internet, why should our front benchers be dictating the topical issue for debate? We should be allowing the public to decide that through internet polls. If we did, the chamber would be far

fuller because we would be discussing the desires of local people who have a direct input into their democracy.

Time and again we have debates in Westminster Hall about
local and regional issues and issues that matter to us. I would
want to move the apparatus of our adjournment debates by
taking them out of the capital to towns and cities throughout the country – whether Gloucester, Bristol, Birmingham
or Manchester – and giving those areas a little prestige by
being part of Parliament. Instead of ministers responding to
debates by reading out sides of A4, I think that you would
find them responding to packed public galleries rather than
to one man and his dog and maybe a lobby correspondent.
We would then also be able to re-engage local media. I think
that it would be a good thing for those ministers to feel the
heat of local public opinion. That is likely to change the culture of decision-making, and would, I think, lead to better
decisions being taken in the first place.

At the current rate of change, we in this House will not be
representative of modern Britain at any stage in the next 100
years. I do not want to be a dictator, I promise you – honestly,
I do – but the next Speaker of this House needs to be a driver
for change, someone who will cajole and try to persuade
our party leaders to make this House more representative
of our different classes, genders and races much, much quicker.
I cannot believe that in 2009 we are still talking about having
a crèche that we members can pay for in this House. If the
next Speaker, whoever he or she is, does not implement that
idea within the next twelve months, frankly, they will have

failed. We need to make fundamental changes. We need a more deferential Parliament. We will be stronger, ultimately, and more respected as politicians if we move the pendulum of power back to local communities.

In conclusion, my father always said while bringing up my two older siblings and me that nobody should put an artificial barrier between us and our hopes, our expectations and our ambitions. That would be a good motto for whoever is the next Speaker of this House because I want people to aspire to be here. I want them to be ambitious, regardless of their background, to create a House that is more representative of modern Britain. If we are not brave enough to make changes here, in the mother of all parliaments, then where? After the time that we have just had – if not now, then when? The rest is up to you.

·   ·   ·

For the record, here is the list of candidates for the Speakership who contested the election that day in the order they spoke:

Dame Margaret Beckett DBE
Sir George Young 6th Baronet
Right Honourable Ann Widdecombe
Sir Alan Beith
Right Honourable John Bercow
Sir Richard Shepherd
Sir Michael Lord

Sir Patrick Cormack

Sir Alan Haselhurst

Parmjit Dhanda

All very likeable people, I must say, and it was a privilege to share the stage with them that day. I don't begrudge any of them their knighthoods and their future peerages – some folk have all the luck!

Speakership hustings

A final footnote on the campaign for the Speakership of the House of Commons: I may not be of the same political calibre or standing as my rivals that day, but both David Cameron and Nick Clegg decided to single out my speech as they welcomed the new Speaker to his seat. I beg your indulgence by including what they said here, partly because it did mean a lot to me but also because maybe it means that, in some way, they did 'get' what I was saying. I hope so. I am also grateful to Gordon Brown for ringing me the following day to express his congratulations.

David Cameron: I listened carefully, as did Hon. Members throughout the House, to an excellent debate this afternoon and a series of very strong and powerful speeches. I thought that there was something very powerful in what the Hon. Member for Gloucester (Mr Dhanda) said about our need to demonstrate in this House of Commons that we get it – that we get the need for transparency, that we get the need for the reform of pay and allowances, and that we get the need to understand, and respond properly to, the public's anger. We share a collective responsibility for what went wrong; we share a collective responsibility for putting it right. Your success will enable all of us to succeed in that; and on that note, I wish you well.

Nick Clegg: In your speech to us this afternoon, you rightly said, 'I do not want to be someone; I want to do something.' I urge you also to remember some of the words of other candidates in today's election, especially those of the Hon. Member for Gloucester (Mr Dhanda) who rightly said that we should all look to change what he called the settlement between Parliament and the people...

CHAPTER 39

A LAMENT FOR THE
FALLEN WARRIORS

THE SIKHS MAY sometimes come across as a bit timid and retiring, but we've had our moments. The faith has had more than its share of blood spilt – with many a historic battle in its 400-year history – hence the 'warrior' tag it so often attracts. Its military history is associated with both the Indian and British armies.

The battling spirit is something the faith is proud of and we do have a habit of reminding ourselves of it in difficult times. In British politics, only a few Sikhs have made it into Parliament, and all of my Sikh Labour contemporaries have now passed away. Currently, the only Sikh MP is the Conservative Paul Uppal, who managed to get elected in Enoch Powell's Wolverhampton constituency in 2010 – no small feat in itself. Lib Dem Parmjit Singh Gill was elected in Leicester South in July 2004 but defeated at the 2005 general election.

On the Labour benches we once had four Sikhs serving in the British Parliament: Piara Khabra in Ealing Southall; Marsha Singh in Bradford; and Tarsem King in the House of Lords. All three were good friends of mine and I have fond memories of them. Obviously I was the fourth member of this quad until my defeat.

We have a tradition of respecting those who came before us so it feels appropriate in the closing chapters of a book about political journeys to lament the fallen warriors. They all had battles to fight to achieve what they did.

Piara Khabra

On getting my job as a Labour Party organiser, I first met Piara in 1996. I couldn't understand how this diminutive little man, barely 5 ft 6 tall and as skinny as a rake, could arouse such emotions. He was revered, feared and lampooned in equal measure.

His first words to me were: 'Hello, young man. I know your father and your grandfather.' He did. He knew everyone. His roots spanned the first generation and their elders.

In Southall he took control of the Indian Workers Association (IWA). My father tells me that he himself was one of its thousands

PARMJIT DHANDA

of members. The IWA was like a trade union for those who had arrived from India to Ealing. Piara had big plans for the IWA.

He joined the Communist Party, the Labour Party, the SDP and came back to the Labour Party as he looked to break into the world of politics. Nobody was going to budge to give him a seat in Parliament so he took one. He used the IWA and a group of first-generation Indian lieutenants to build a Labour Party membership that would overwhelm the incumbent Labour MP in Southall – Sidney Bidwell. All this happened under the noses of the NEC and the Labour establishment. They just didn't know how to react. Labour's leader Neil Kinnock was an Ealing resident at the time.

Piara, for many, was a figure of fun. But to take his destiny and that of the IWA into his own hands was an extraordinary feat. The more members he recruited the more his opponents did likewise, but they couldn't keep up with him. His ascent to Bidwell's crown was unstoppable. Through fear, loyalty and skill, a party of 5,000 members (a typical party wouldn't have a tenth of that) carried him to his selection. The Labour Party nationally collected the subs knowing full well many of the members had not paid for their own membership (and some did not even know they were members). After all, was a white, left-of-centre party going to block its only Indian-born MP? It could not.

He had a strategy. He worked through lieutenants who recruited for him (about five of them) and some had junior recruiters who in turn recruited for them. The lieutenants became councillors and were taken aside and promised by Piara that they would one day succeed him. He would keep them all guessing and played them off against each other.

He was impossible to control. When I asked him to keep a low profile and not to say anything controversial in the run-up to the 1997 election, he agreed. Later that week he featured on the front page of the *Ealing Gazette* with the headline: 'MP slams opponents as bastards and idiots.' He followed it up a few weeks later with one suggesting India should 'nuke' Pakistan. It was never boring working with him.

He could speak for hours and sometimes the words didn't come out as planned. I recall him saying to an audience: 'In Southall politics, yesterday's enemy is today's friend. And today's friend is tomorrow's enemy.' That wiped a few smiles off some faces. It was an apt description of Southall politics in its day.

In many ways he was a political giant. As time goes on, I do find his achievement increasingly remarkable.

Marsha Singh

As we got closer to the 10 p.m. vote, Marsha's Punjabi got louder and louder in the division lobbies. He'd often greet me with a loud '*Kiddha*!' and a slap on my back. We'd then trade a few phrases in the mother tongue to leave other MPs looking perplexed – just because we could! Marsha was chair of his local constituency party in Bradford where he was selected. It was a seat with a big Muslim community and large Muslim Labour Party membership. He did very well to come through his selection and he negotiated a path through tricky community politics. His local popularity was strengthened by the marathon of casework surgeries he ran. They were drop-ins so he would see everyone who came. He once told me about a five-hour Saturday surgery session he had run.

Sadly, the death of his first wife hit him very hard. I often wonder whether Parliament could have done more to support him when troubled times struck. His health suffered and he resigned his seat. He then died just a few months later. Far too young.

Tarsem King

Tarsem was leader of Sandwell Council and soon became Lord King of Sandwell. He first came to my attention at an event at Millbank in the late 1990s where he was one of the speakers. I had heard of him but he wasn't what I was expecting – older, first generation and very softly spoken. He was never going to make great waves and become a household name; it wasn't his style. That day at Millbank, in his calm manner, he told an ethnic minority Labour Party audience to stop chasing the shiny chains of civic office. He said the trouble with our people (ethnic minorities) was that when we were involved in politics we were obsessed with becoming ceremonial mayors rather than council leaders or portfolio holders. I could hear mayoral chains rustling around me with indignation. He was right, of course, and when I went up and told him so afterwards, a friendship began that lasted until his death in 2013.

My father and I would visit him whenever we were in the West Midlands. He was very close friends with my father's uncle and they both attended my wedding with their families. When I was elected, we'd meet for tea to discuss how our respective families were growing and he would give me the benefit of his political wisdom. Quietly spoken he may have been, but he had strong views and told me who I should or shouldn't trust.

He lived a good, honest life. When he died he left a huge gap in the community's representation in Parliament and he left me as the last survivor of what was once a growing Sikh political Labour family.

CHAPTER 40

MY LAST WORD

W E'VE COME FULL circle now. Defeat was painful. And then came the pig's head incident. Some months later I received an email from Natascha Engel MP. She was heading an all-party group that wanted to do an inquiry into behaviours at elections and was particularly interested to know if my family or I had experienced racism during election campaigns.

I realised I had accumulated a generation of experiences in my life that I had kept brushed away under the rug – too proud to talk about some of them; too wary of the political consequences to talk about others. And too embarrassed about being seen as different. As a brown face in a white seat, someone who had been heralded as an example of how things could be – and how they *should* be – I didn't want to shatter any of those illusions.

Campaigning in 2010

So I wrote a note to the all-party group and highlighted a few of the things that had happened along the way. I was surprised at how stunned they were by some of the content. They asked me to give evidence in person. By then I was starting to miss the old place and couldn't resist the chance to go back to a parliamentary committee room to give my evidence. Giving evidence was a cathartic experience for me. Marie Woolf of the *Sunday Times* heard about the pig's head and wrote about it in the newspaper.

It made me think. I didn't want people to feel sorry for me, but I also wanted to share my experiences so others would know more about the challenges still faced today by people who are 'different' in politics. Maybe it might help a few underdogs along the way, or at least encourage parties to provide them with a safety net.

I hope you have found from reading this book that mine is not a story of misery and woe. Some wonderful things happened to me and I've met some amazing people along the way. Most importantly for a politician, I've made many people's lives better. If I've made you laugh a bit along the way, so much the better still. I hope all political parties will feel there's something in here worth taking on board.

In many respects, this story was not about my political race. It has been shaped by the experiences of my parents, who came here to work and to earn in the 1960s. It's been their journey as much as mine and I have very much enjoyed researching their lives, seeing the world through their eyes and understanding what drove me to do the things I did.

So, what's next? People ask me quite often if I'll ever return to politics. All I can say is read the book again and decide for yourself how hard it would be for somebody like me. The stats suggest it hasn't got any easier – and my recent experiences suggest that too. In any case, I'm in a settled place now. The two red boxes from my ministerial days house the kids' football boots and the black one from the Whips' Office holds my wife's make-up.

My political race is probably run – but just one parting piece of advice remains. Whatever your background or faith (if you have one or not), when your back is against the wall – or people say no and want to block your path – get in touch with what I call 'your inner Sikh'. It's the bit of you that won't back down and won't take no for an answer. And, as long as mine is still in me, well, you never quite know. Maybe one day...

ACKNOWLEDGEMENTS

THANK YOU TO Biteback Publishing for sharing my passion for this project from the very beginning and to Iain Dale for saying in 2009 that I deserved to be Speaker of the House for having the nicest tie. It ensured that Biteback would be my first port of call when *My Political Race* was just an idea.

I'm grateful to everyone who has featured in this book. Without them, this body of work would not have come together as an entity. I apologise to the many people who could have featured in this book but who haven't: friends, family, colleagues and comrades. There's always more that could have been said, or tales that could have been recalled, but *My Political Race* was never meant to be a marathon.

Thank you to my family for being the extraordinary people that they are. This is their story as much as it is mine.

None of this would have happened if it weren't for the backing of the Gloucester CLP. They were my conscience at Westminster and my strength in the constituency – and regularly our babysitters, too.

To my Westminster, constituency and campaign staff over the nine years we worked together: David Purchase, Tricia Delaney, Helen Newton, Theo Bertram, Stuart Hudson, Kamella Hudson, Chris Turner, Paul Nicholson, Emily Georghiou, James Green, Matt Kelcher, Keith Corley, Lucy Jenkins, Matthew Gilson and Sarah Norman. I know how lucky I was to have you in my corner; thank you for making me look good.

And, finally, to the people of Gloucester – you proved a lot of people wrong about human nature and I hope political parties will learn from that. It was a privilege to represent you.

INDEX